acclaim for kelee katillac and house of belief:

"House of Belief inspires at every turn."

- Claire Whitcomb, *Chicago Tribune/Universal Press*

"This is a remarkable story of a woman who says a home is more than a place that stores your things; that it is a place where a child feels loved and supported. And, a place that supports and reflects who they are and who they want to be...Kelee Katillac...House of Belief...it's beautiful."

- Oprah Winfrey from the *Oprah Winfrey Show*

"Unlike the 'seamless' designers, Katillac likes the notion of the bedroom as a sacred domain for kids."

- Shawn Sell, *USA Today*

"...an exceptional book which tells how to incorporate one's personality and beliefs in a home decoration style."

- *Midwest Book Review*

"Kelee Katillac helps clients shape their beliefs as she transforms their houses."

- *Rocky Mountain News*

KIDS' SACRED PLACES

rooms for believing & belonging

I am becoming...

KIDS' SACRED PLACES

rooms for believing & belonging

by **Kelee Katillac**

PHOTOGRAPHS BY ROY INMAN

ICE PRESS

WHERE CREATIVITY IS COOL!

KANSAS CITY, MISSOURI

House of Belief™ is a trademark of Kelee Katilllac
ICE PRESS™ is a trademark of The Institute for Creativity Empowerment
Heart and Hands™ Process, Make & Believe™ and Belief-Based Decorating™
are trademarks of Kelee Katillac

Library of Congress
Cataloging-in-Publication Data

Katillac, Kelee.
Kids' sacred places : rooms for believing and belonging / by Kelee Katillac
p. cm.
Includes bibliographical references and index.
ISBN 0-9770390-0
1. Children's rooms. 2. Interior decoration—Psychological aspects. 3. Parent and child.
I. Title.

NK2117.C4 K38 2003
747.7'7—dc21
2002034108

PRINTED IN THE UNITED STATES OF AMERICA

08 07 06 05   4 3 2 1
FIRST EDITION

BOOK DESIGN BY CHARLES MCSTRAVICK
EDITORIAL SUPERVISION BY CHAD EDWARDS
EDITORIAL SUPPORT BY DAVID R. MACAULAY AND JOE GODEK
BOOK PRODUCTION BY MARIO M. RODRIGUEZ, MMR DESIGN SOLUTIONS
PRINTING BY PHOENIX COLOR

ICEPRESS
P.O. Box 7128
Kansas City, Missouri 64113
Phone: 816-256-7012
www.ice-press.com

Dedicated to

my childhood family:

Jerry,

Judy,

Scott,

Mabel,

Norman,

Mary,

&

Neil

acknowledgements . . .

. . . to my dear husband, Steve, a heart-full thank you for your unending support, encouragement, and belief.

. . . to Mary Pipher, PhD (author of *Reviving Ophelia*), for her ground-breaking work in family therapy. She has inspired me to make a therapeutic connection between creativity and family healing.

. . . to *House of Belief* readers, practitioners, devotees, creative healers, and the courageously creative who have contacted me and are doing this and similar good work worldwide.

. . . to my friends and colleagues whose words of wisdom and encouragement, creative gifts and cards at just the right moments, and whose brilliant expressions of the Creative Spirit in their own lives continually empower me to do more and work harder.

. . . to my talented photographer and friend Roy Inman.

. . . to the hundreds of volunteers nationwide who have participated in the Community House of Belief Pilot workshops.

. . . to my support team: Arielle Ford, Brian Hilliard, Debbie Luican, Chad Edwards, Sandy D'Amato, Sara Frank, Christine Garvey, Dick Henderson, Susan Andrews, Kathy Wismer,

Steve Larson, Jamie Rich, Shana Weinberg, Reverend Duke Tufty, Reverend Karyn Bradley, Reverend Chris Michaels, Matt Nichols, the late Katie McNeil, and early on Joan and Jack Ryan, Rose Garner, Cathi Horton, and Victoria Moran.

. . . to my assistant, Lois Benge-Fortin, whose integrity, loyalty and positive nature make our work possible.

. . . especially, to the school teachers, educators, and librarians who do similar good work year-in and year-out. Also, art therapists everywhere for your support of my work. These facilitators are all too often taken for granted. Thank you for your dedication – we need you.

. . . to the the faith-based groups that have helped to pilot this book including: the Catholic Campaign for Human Development; Unity Churches of Kansas City and Chicago; and Habitat for Humanity International.

. . . to Hallmark Cards' Kaleidoscope Creative Center for their early involvement in introducing *Kids' Sacred Places*.

. . . to those in the media who have shined a light on this important work, including: Oprah Winfrey; Oxygen Network; *USA Today;* Universal Press Syndicate; *Body and Soul;* Christopher Lowell; Caroline Myss; *The Utne Reader; Designer/Builder Magazine;* and every newspaper and other media outlet that has helped us to share this message throughout the universe.

CHAPTER FOUR: Two warring step-sisters learn to forgive, share, and even become friends through this heart and hands decorating project. A Gerber Daisy was added to the wall for each of the girls' positive actions.

CONTENTS

INTRODUCTION

Acceptance, understanding, and love given unconditionally—these are the resounding themes of the real-life storybook you have in your hands. The storytellers—kids writing their own stories and bringing them into form within their homes—are also its heroes and heroines. In their "sacred places," good always triumphs over evil.

In *Kids' Sacred Places*, the hands are at the service of the heart, shaping homes into sacred vessels containing the good intentions of all who live there. In what I call the "House of Belief" work, home becomes a fortress with foundation stones of personal creativity, belief, and belonging. Throughout this book, you will see evidence that somehow the kids' imagined worlds have become real, expressed through handmade chairs, pillows, curtains, and walls (yes, these walls can talk) that reflect the noble heart-felt intentions of the young and old spirits from which they came.

You will find that like any good story, our cast of characters is complete, and our plot a classic. Not only are there heroes and heroines, but there are also those people and situations that are antagonistic to our self-beliefs. These negative forces abound in the world, and unfortunately it can be difficult to keep them from entering our homes. The chorus of young voices pleading for help want a safe and sacred place of retreat.

For instance, a young boy in California came home one day to find that some kids from his high school had penetrated the walls of his home. They had broken in and desecrated his

DRESS REHEARSAL: The childhood process of dress-up allows kids to rehearse for life, trying on a character's intentions, beliefs, and values. In Ardis Petersen's neighborhood, the kids, some of whom are underprivileged, get to role-play a better life. Griselda is a peace-loving princess; Alair a good-hearted fairy godmother; Georgina a willful gypsy; Alex a noble knight; and Leah a mustached magician.

bedroom, destroying the objects he had made in his shop class at school. They wrote cruel names on the walls and even tore apart his bed. It seemed he had no escape from the endless taunts of the foes that deemed him "too different." They didn't like his hair, his parent's car, or the way he talked. A year or two before, they had begun their barrage by tearing down the tree house he had made.

Like all kids, he had creatively attempted to "make" a world of his own inside his home. What happened to him is nearly beyond our comprehension and is, no doubt, complex. The details aside, the boy fell into a fight for his very life. Not long after that final assault on his spirit and creativity, via his bedroom, he took an irreversible action. The result was a death toll at his high school only slightly less than at Columbine High School in Colorado. In effect, those "evildoers" had taken his power and made him one of their own. With tragic stories like this one becoming more prevalent, something needed to be done. Our heroes and heroines have been doing it: putting creativity into action to make sacred places of belief and belonging.

One heroine in the battle to keep our homes and self-images intact has touched the lives of millions of people with her uplifting and empowering vision. As you can imagine, I was truly honored when the producers of the *Oprah Winfrey Show* called and asked me to share my House of Belief work with Oprah and her audience. The producers had been looking for a guest with information that could provide a way for children and parents to combat the negative influences in our everyday lives—playground bullies, gossips, and hurtful beliefs—and I was recommended. They felt that my House of Belief philosophy of interior transformation of the home and spirit was just the sort of positive message for which they were looking. It was this favorable response that encouraged me to write this book.

Working with me over the last two years of case study, the kids, families, and friends in these inspiring chapters are writing their own stories, and hand-making their own worlds. The objects we have created together are representative of their heart intentions for life: beliefs, values, goals, and dreams—those ideas that will help them through the loneliest times and the darkest moments.

Here are just a few to inspire you:

❋ Rebeka, 15, celebrates her values of faith, love, family, friendship, and future with painted pillows and walls strewn with her joyful tissue paper confetti. Her mom, Cherie, 49, loosens her traditional concepts about decorating to embrace her own childlike creativity by finding her *True Colors*.

- Alex, 10, who has been relentlessly picked on by school bullies, looks to great men who overcame childhood adversity and went on to live heroic lives. He makes an *In-Memory Lamp* project with his heroes' pictures applied to encourage him forward.

- Jessica, 13, and her mom, Jodi, 35, have discovered a process to help them let go of unkind thoughts and negative words through a *Re-Upolstering Me Chair* project. They re-upholster their worn-out thoughts and chairs alike with uplifting colors and positive words and symbols.

- Jasmine, 12, brings a foundation to her goal of becoming a writer by painting her stories and book cover designs on the floor beneath her feet. Her story, *Just Like Me*, shares profound ideas about racism and equality.

- Henry, 7, who is coping with divorce, makes a *Safe-in-Bedspread* project to provide a feeling of security at night. He draws chickens from his dad's farm to later apply to his curtains so that images he associates with his dad remain in view.

- Aunt Jeanette, 55, helps to welcome her newly adopted niece baby Anna into the family by making a *Love Letter Blanket* project with her new parents' tender words about how they feel to have her in their lives.

- Anna, 9, and Alexis, 11, who are sisters through re-marriage, overcome their jealousy and unkindness by making a *Flower-Empower Decorated Wall* project. A flower is added to the wall pattern to represent their individual acts of kindness; the pattern is thereby made up of their loving actions.

These courageous kids and families, as well as many others in this real-life storybook, demonstrate how to make personal sanctuaries, where young spirits can joyfully grow and believe and thrive. Theirs is a creative land where they have the power to make with their hands whatever they imagine. As they paint, craft, and create into being their intentions about life within their homes, we come to realize that the real sanctuary they are making is within themselves.

✳✳✳

CHAPTER 1

born believing

We are all born animate vessels of belief and creativity. Like beret-wearing, paintbrush-wielding ginger jars come to life, we ourselves are a work of art and an artist—both created and creative. In the same way we may share Mom's baby blues and Dad's noble jaw line, we also share our Creator's creativity. It is in our spiritual genetics, just as eye color or height is passed to us from our earthly parents. Flowing through our spirits like blood in our bodies is the creative urge to colorfully imagine and dream, and the unwavering belief that we can create what we have envisioned. If creativity is the vital fluid of Spirit, then belief is certainly the heart that pumps it. And children are birthed, I believe, in excellent spiritual health.

Just ask any classroom of first graders—Who can make their family dinner or help a needy person go to college or act in a play or fly to the moon or paint a picture or compete in the Olympics?—and you'll see as many crayon-stained palms waving overhead as there are kids at desks. Then ask each of them to draw a picture of themselves doing one of the stated activities. Delighted to have an immediate hands-on action to express the belief of their nearly

THEATER OF MAKE & BELIEVE: This attic dormer has been painted into a Theater of Make & Believe: a playroom where neighborhood children can use their imagination, and costumes, to dress rehearse for life.

1

bursting hearts, they go to work illustrating their vision. Their hands become the tools of their hearts, conduits for inner ideas—beliefs, values, goals, and dreams for life. They paint or draw or craft or paste their dream into form. They make it so they can believe in it—and themselves. This success encourages another action of creativity, which in turn builds more belief. This belief contributes to the positive self-identity of the child and accompanies them wherever they may go in life.

Five-year-old Deborah had her belief with her on the day I met her at the coffee shop I frequent. Her dad was also a regular and familiar to me, but Deborah quickly became a brand new friend. "I can make *anything* from paper—I made Hanukkah decorations for my room," she said, pausing to take a big draw of her hot chocolate through a straw and adjust her hot pink hat. Then she continued, "Hanukkah means I believe in God's Ten Commandments. I can also swim on my back underwater and on my side too, but really I am mostly an artist."

The famous painter Pablo Picasso's statement, "Every child is an artist, the problem is how to remain one as we grow up" agreed with her. The quote implies, though, that there is something that happens during childhood and beyond that cracks away at the vessels of belief and creativity we were at the beginning. With cracks in the vessel, how can the creativity remain within? Early in childhood, the substance of creativity can actually keep those first fissures in our self-esteem from widening; by flowing into inner wounds, providing a healing mortar.

Every semester, Mrs. Petersen invited a costumed character to her third-grade class. Once it was a pioneer, another time it was a policeman. This year it was a sad clown. The character would talk about who they are and why they look the way they do; what their clothing symbolizes; and what they represent in the world. Then she would ask the children to draw a picture of the character. She hadn't anticipated the power of one rendering by a boy named Brian.

First, you must understand that Brian was a regular third grade boy. He threw spit wads, pulled girls' hair, made endearing cards for his mom, and lamented spelling tests. Yet, Brian had been born with a withered arm, a short little appendage that made him different. When he presented his rendering of the sad clown to the teacher, she was stunned. The character in his drawing also had a withered arm. Brian had so identified with the plight of the lonely jester that he had made the character to appear just like himself.

Yes, our creativity can be a wonderful healing elixir—a magic potion so powerful that a dose can turn pain into beauty, positive ideas into actions, and dreams into reality. Deborah and Brian are evidence of this truth. It is heart-wrenchingly sad to imagine either of these kids someday less buoyant in their creative beliefs. But if we revisited that same classroom of kids only much later in high school, and posed the same questions about their potential, we would likely receive far different responses. Few would dare to make such an outward expression of belief in themselves and their inherent abilities as they did at age seven.

What happens to us? And more importantly, how do we keep it from happening to our children? Is it possible to keep our belief and creativity intact? What can a parent do to empower a child? These are some of the same questions posed to me by the producers of a television show on which I appeared in a segment about nurturing childhood self-belief. Most people think nurturing our children creatively within our homes has to be complicated and time consuming. I have good news for everyone: It does not have to be! The *Kids' Sacred Places* process is as simple as a game of *make and believe.*

Brian, a boy with a withered arm, drew himself as a sad clown.

make and believe

Over a half century before Harry Potter was "born" to J.K. Rowling, writer C.S. Lewis created four amazing children of his own. In Lewis's series, *The Chronicles of Narnia,* we follow their mystical adventures that begin in a big English house owned by an eccentric old professor:

It was the sort of house that you never seem to come to the end of, and it was full of unexpected places. The first few doors they tried led only to spare bedrooms, as everyone had expected they would; but soon they came to a very long room full of pictures and armor . . . and then came three steps down and five steps up . . . and then a whole series of rooms that led into each other and were lined with books . . . and shortly after that they looked into a room that was quite empty except for one big wardrobe . . . .

One by one, the fictional kids—Edmund, Lucy, Peter, and Susan—climb into the English wardrobe cabinet and push through layer after layer of clothing to find a doorway to a mystical land called Narnia. The noble ruler of this place is a majestic lion named Aslan. They encounter other legendary creatures like unicorns, fauns, and centaurs. Their adventures in this place are limited only to their belief in its existence. In the story, the children are confronted by situations that challenge their personal beliefs and ethics. Believing, however, isn't enough. They must take action on their beliefs and stand up for what is right. When they reach adulthood they can no longer enter this idyllic land because, they are told, adults no longer truly believe.

The series of seven stories is a great example of what I call the process of *make and believe*—not to be confused with make-believe in which everything is assumed to be only play. Make and then *believe* is a creative process by which what we imagine and then make visible through costumes and room decorations begins to be believable. As in the Harry Potter books (which we will talk more about later), we understand that magic isn't really some external power that we must conjure or acquire from another source. It is just another word for the power of belief and creativity that lives inside of us all. And the dark forces—dragons, demons, and trolls—that we all encounter, parents and kids alike, are really everyday foes: peer pressure; family issues like divorce; bullies at school or work; low self-esteem and negative personal beliefs. When you begin to understand this storybook language, it is easy to see how we all—not just our children—can live triumphant, storybook lives.

the wardrobe closet

In a working-class neighborhood near the railroad tracks and beside a river that runs through an industrial corridor of a small city, a former art teacher has opened a magical wardrobe door on a better world for all who know her. It seems that Lewis's story has

COMMUNITY CREATIVITY: Ardis Petersen and her friends Tommie Baughman, Jeanette Evans-Hamilton, and Kelly Edmister decorated a spare room in her home with references to positive children's stories. Here, any child can act out noble themes and become a hero.

come to real-life. Within her Victorian-era home—an uncanny match for the old professor's house—Mrs. Ardis Petersen calls upon the power of the costumed character. In a high-up attic dormer, she has created an otherworldly stage on which the neighborhood children, many of whom are from low-income and underprivileged families, can come and escape the harsh realities of the world they know. As they dig deep into her costume closet and their own creative spirits, they gain entry to a land very much like Narnia, a place where they can become anything they believe. With great excitement they make their own costumes and characters. And as they step onto the stage of imagination, they see more in themselves than they may have ever been told to believe was possible.

Ardis, whose wonderful home is surrounded by flowers she planted herself, finds that working with the neighbor children is rather like planting a community garden:

Kids need personal belief, love and respect for themselves and others. The kinds of skills the kids learn through acting and drama provide those things. For example, you must learn to be dependable and finish a project—no matter what, you must persevere until you complete your goal. They also develop poise and self-confidence from being in front of people. These qualities will help them succeed in a work environment later in life. I plant these seeds. Sometimes I see them bloom, and other times I know that they will take hold and change their lives as adults. When you are nurturing people and plants, you have to be patient.

I first met this remarkable lady when she participated in one of my House of Belief workshops. She became a true believer in this process and was interested in making a House of Belief community workshop in her neighborhood. As I learned more about her and spent time in her home, a plan evolved.

Ardis had not only been an art teacher, but also a community leader as well—presenting backyard circuses, neighborhood shows, and Community Theater. When we met, she was working on a production to be staged at a local church. In her home, this mother of five and grandmother of eight offered the disenfranchised kids on her street a safe haven for fun and learning in her attic playroom. Many of them, from ages 4 to 17, had nowhere to go after school or when it was cold outside. Some even needed refuge from neighborhood dangers: bullies, ill-intentioned strangers, and domestic violence. Most of their good parents, however, were simply working so hard to make ends meet, they just didn't have much time to spend with their children.

THE FROG PRINCESS: Griselda's mom says that the theater playroom stimulates her daughter's imagination and gives her many creative ideas that she brings home to her own room.

Why not, I suggested, make the current attic playroom into a *Theater of Make & Believe*? A sacred place to throw open the wardrobe closet of possibility for these children and inspire their hearts and minds? And as she gathered together others from my workshops and friends from her community who wanted to be involved in creating such a place, the ideas were abundant. Key volunteers Jeanette Evans-Hamilton, Tommie Baughman and Kelly Edmister envisioned that a bunk bed could be a balcony for Romeo and Juliet or a place for Rapunzel to let down her hair . . . over there a chaise for any generic fainting princess . . . in there a castle keep for armor . . . a wardrobe closet for . . . . Yes, even the adults were rekindling their childlike creativity, and here is how you can, too.

getting started: heart and hands projects

The hardest part about getting started is moving past our adult expectations and limitations: adult expectations about what decorating a house should be like and limiting thoughts about our own capacities for creativity. As a "reformed" interior designer, I constantly remind myself to decorate from the heart, rather than from the pages of magazines espousing the latest style. Even after years of practicing this philosophy of *belief-based decorating,* the media can still influence me, tempting me to decorate for approval. With our children's beliefs and creativity at stake, we begin to understand the danger to our kids of parents yielding to such impulses. I'll address both of these extensively in coming chapters, giving you the support you'll need to decorate from the heart.

Throughout *Kids' Sacred Places* we will use *heart and hands projects* as a vehicle for meaningfully decorating our family spaces. Simply, a heart and hands project is taking a positive idea from your heart and making something about it with your hands. The invisible contents of the heart become visible, and when we see it we believe in it. This heart-felt meaning is what distinguishes a heart and hands project from a "craft project." There is no truer saying than "a picture is worth a thousand words"—or a chair or a pillow or a curtain, or even a wardrobe costume closet made by you and your children. By introducing these meaningful projects to your child, you present him or her with creative actions to help express positive intentions and beliefs, values, goals, and dreams for life. I invite you to try the guided creative activities that

Artist Tommie Baughman used his heart and hands to turn a cast-off chair into a small throne, and Jeanette Evans-Hamilton added to the atmosphere by painting castle walls. In the process, the two helped turn displaced kids into kings and queens.

are included in each chapter of this book with your child, and with your own heart intentions in mind. Remember, what works for our kids works just as well for us, too.

In each of the coming chapters, before each heart and hands project, I will present you with exercises and/or questions to get you and the kids started. These activities will help you find your ideas, heart intentions, and inspiration for the things you create together. Let's get started on creating your own place for make and believe. Group projects are a great place to start—they take the pressure off our adult tendencies toward perfectionism and help us to enlist family and friends who have creative experiences that may be added to our own. Most of all, it's important to fully engage the kids in the process by keeping their creativity and just having some good old-fashioned fun in mind.

costuming your characters

Right now we are only concerned about letting our hair down—or pinning it up—because that's what you do when you wear a wig. There is nothing like the transformative power of the costume closet and a bag full of wigs. With just three wigs in my own magical wardrobe closet, I have been known to conjure up as many as 10 different characters, including the wilted Branson starlet Mavis Monroe—Marilyn's country cousin (for my husband's birthday); Afraditty, an eastern "gaddess of love," all the way from New "Joysea" (for a Valentine's Day party for my lovelorn friends); Eleanor Roosevelt (to illustrate dignity and leadership for a kids workshop); humorist Will Rogers; and the fictional Tolkien character, Bilbo Baggins the Hobbit—both for other workshop endeavors. How's that for a roster? Friends and family, especially my seven-year-old grandson Henry, love to *make and believe* with my costumes, too.

The cast and crew at Ardis's Theater of Make & Believe are very intentional about the costumes and characters they create, in the same way that I donned the persona of Eleanor Roosevelt to illustrate the positive attributes of dignity and leadership, and the Hobbit Bilbo Baggins to talk about cowardice, courage, and purpose. They create costumes for characters whose attributes they know, love, admire, respect, or despise; characters who teach us something when we wear their costume. For example, Little Bo Peep is cautious; a Bumble Bee is a hard worker; Harry Potter is brave and intelligent; Abe Lincoln represents honor and integrity.

✳   Think of stories of the characters you loved as a child, and those your kids love today. Reference your favorite books, movies and plays. Even think about people, in the news, or celebrities. What can we learn from them? What do their costumes look like? Make a list on a separate piece of paper.

✳   Now, think of favorite places and settings from books, movies, plays, or real life. Describe how they feel, smell, and look. What materials can you think of to make up your own version? You need not make the whole set. Focus on the area where your favorite action in the story happens. For example, it could be in *Superman* when Clark Kent jumps into the telephone booth to "become" his powerful self. A telephone booth could be made—a place to become stronger. Now, write down your ideas.

✳   Is there a place somewhere in your home to make your own little wardrobe closet or Theater of Make & Believe? What is the difference between the two? A wardrobe closet

COSTUMES OF CHARACTER: Collect costume pieces or make your own. Be sure to label them with the character traits associated with the costume; this provides opportunity for discussions about beliefs, values, and intentions.

can be tucked into a working closet or created from an old cabinet or chest. A theater will require a little more space and time but need not be too elaborate. It can be in the attic or basement, a corner nook in the family room, a child's bedroom, or even in the garage. Taking time to feed your child's imagination will be worth it. Griselda's mom agrees:

When Griselda comes home from Ardis's house, she wants to paint and draw. When I ask her where her ideas come from, she says playing make-believe in the castle room gives her many ideas.

creating "costumes of character"

A costume closet or theater in your home can stimulate your child's imagination about the greater possibilities of life, giving them the creative capacity to make their dreams come true. It also provides great learning opportunities for parents as well, offering a unique way for everyone to find all that is within them. Alair, one of the kids from Ardis's neighborhood, exclaimed upon entering the Theater of Make & Believe, "It is a dream come true!" Isn't that what all parents want to do for their children, give them the power to make their dreams come true? This project will help.

HEART AND HANDS PROJECT

heart objective: To stimulate curiosity, imagination, and understanding. Through dress-up role-playing we become aware of the qualities, good and bad, that are represented in real-life role models and storybook characters alike.

hands activity: Using the above examples, identify four different characters that your child admires and would like to emulate. Make their costumes from what you have or from the other resources listed in the "Making It Real" section. Make tags for each of the costumes. List the qualities in that character that you admire. You can add more costumes as time permits. Then, store the costumes in a *wardrobe closet*. Make your own using an old refrigerator box or cardboard moving wardrobe.

A portable costume closet can be fashioned from a recycled cardboard appliance box.

as you go forward

Here are a few guidelines for creating kids' places that are empowering. First, think of all the neighbors, family, and friends who might help you. Those with creative skills like sewing or painting would be very helpful. As the group—whether it's just you and the kids or others you have enlisted—begins to make and believe together, try not to be too thematic. For example, making a whole space all about one story, like say, *The Frog Prince,* with frogs painted everywhere, could be limiting to the kids' imaginations. Creating rooms that are all on one subject can be like locking your child into that one storybook. A child's room needs to stimulate thoughts of a million worlds, not just one. We want to open up the imagination, not bind it with our own adult whims.

A room that is too thematic is like a shiny toy at Christmas—the kids love it for about an hour and then discard it for a broomstick and a shoebox. After all, a shoebox can be a treasure chest, a doll bed, a cookie jar, a hat, or a jewelry box; and a broomstick becomes a horse, an airplane, a teeter-totter, or a trombone. Note how Ardis's group made spaces that could belong in many different stories: a balcony, a princess bed, a castle, and so on.

In creating your place for make and believe, I recommend these creative guidelines:

❋ Use what you have on hand or that which you can scavenge from the neighbors, yard sales, thrift stores, or the curb.

❋ Limit your budget. Necessity is the mother of invention and imagination.

❋ Budget your time as well. If you are short on time, as so many are these days, a meaningful wardrobe closet could actually be made on a Saturday morning. When your time is up, the kids will cherish the morning you spent with them. You can have more special outings together, looking for additional costume pieces, in the future.

❋ Budgeting allowances on time and money will keep you working spontaneously and keep adult insistences about "doing it right" to a minimum.

❋ In most cases, when working on heart and hands projects, it is advisable to incorporate the manufacturer's instructions on any tools or supplies you may have purchased.

❋ Dressing in character needn't be part of a formal play. Get dressed up for fun (and learning) just to have dinner together.

❋ Be sure to always emphasize the "heart" part of any heart and hands project. It is the most meaningful part of your experience.

CHAPTER 2

a hero's tale

In the last chapter, Ardis's little group of ragtag actors demonstrated the concept of *make and believe.* The wardrobe cabinet served as a passageway to an empowering land—a place of imagination within each child. Now, we move on to incorporate this make and believe process into the real-life "character development" of our children. In the theater of our homes, we are in rehearsal for the larger dramas of life. We get to choose the role we play, and its grandeur is limited only to our *creative belief:* the ability to use our creativity to make it all happen. The lessons our children learn on the tiny, mutable stage of their bedrooms can become a positive force in the scenes they play out as adults.

At seven years old, I knew exactly who I was and my bedroom reflected it. Outward expressions of my interests, values, goals, and dreams were everywhere. Art materials ranged from a favorite liquid embroidery kit that I had received as a gift at my dad's company Christmas party, to the jewelry beads and ropes and colorful tissues for origami sculptures I had acquired in other kits. I loved those creativity packages. Every new acquisition filled my heart with promise—there was more that I could be and accomplish. As I looked upon the tea towels embellished with liquid thread patterns or wore necklaces of my own design, my self-

HEART AND HANDS PROJECTS: In Henry's bedroom he expresses the contents of his heart: his love of his dogs and his dad's farm, by using his hands to create areas and objects to represent them. Jackie Denning helped Henry create a headboard, bedspread, and curtains about these meaningful ideas.

17

esteem was bolstered. Also, I was self-reliant. I could make what I needed, or as in the case of my pony, I had literally *believed* something into being.

At an early age I had learned the power of seeing and believing, using actions and affirmations to manifest the things I wanted in life. By age two, I had started to visualize a pony in my parents' small barn. Then, I took it a step further. When visitors arrived, I would ask if they would like to see my pony—I had added a candy-striped stick horse with a lush yarn mane and tail to the stall of the barn. His little head hung perfectly over the manger, perpetually munching fresh hay. This ritual repeated itself with every new arrival at my house. I believed that one day that stick horse would become real. On the evening of my third birthday, as a crowd of family and friends gathered in my parents' living room, I was ordered to go to my bedroom. When I was invited to return to the party, I was sure I had fallen asleep on my bed and was dreaming, once again, my favorite dream. Right there, in the middle of my parents' living room, stood a tiny Shetland pony colt!

Even now, the memory has a dreamlike quality. How could this happen? A pony? And in the house, too? Logical answers defied comprehension. It seems my granddad had transported her in the back of his station wagon from the farm where she was born. The foal might as well have been dropped out of the air by Peter Pan himself. It seemed I had literally believed and acted her into being! Appropriately, I named her Tinkerbell, and the fairy dust she sprinkled has led to a lifelong enchantment with horses. In the short term, that meant cowboy hats, boots, horse show ribbons, horse statues, posters, and books on every wall and stick of furniture in my bedroom. My self-reliance established, I started working at age 12 to help pay for the riding events. Kids from working-class families can't usually afford this sport. But with the help of my folks and some hard work and ingenuity, we made it happen. By the time I reached college, I sold my horse to help pay for my education.

In the sacred place of my bedroom I saw evidence of the possible. Objects I had made or earned, from jewelry to show ribbons, represented something positive and uplifting about my life. The childhood decorating process of "make and then *believe*" offers us evidence that we are born with the sacred power of the Creator operating within us. Intuitively, I used my imagination to see the things I longed for and loved. Then, in my bedroom, I brought my ideas into form, literally handmaking my dreams into reality. These included science fair projects I created, riding clothes I sewed, carnival games I made and hosted to benefit muscular dystrophy

Author at age 7

MAKE AND BELIEVE: The author learned the power of creative visualization as a small child, making believe she had a pony, until one day it actually appeared in her parents' living room.

research, and ceramic statues painted in a neighbor's basement studio. Ideas and objects I had seen in my imagination became real through my own positive thoughts and actions.

No one taught me this process; I was simply born believing in myself. This belief was nurtured by the creative materials that were provided by my supportive parents. Through the art kit projects, I became skilled in the use of the Creator's kind process for us: to see it in our imagination, to make it with our hands and then to believe it in our hearts. The positive outcome of actually manifesting my dream made me believe even more. Seeing is believing. For a time after that I would tackle any desire with the same self-belief.

In the coming years, though, I was to face a brutal hazing by mean neighborhood kids—and the burden of "giftedness" that made me all too different. At times I felt like an outcast. However, when I looked around my bedroom, I was assured that this was a place where I truly *belonged.* I am convinced that it was this early adeptness at using creative action to build my belief that has helped me through the darkest moments of my adult life: loss of loved ones, illness, and financial struggles. The self-reliance, confidence, and courage I built early on have emboldened me even to take heroic action to help our world.

HENRY'S WORLD: Henry created his own view on the world: curtains stenciled with chickens from his dad's farm. His friend Julie Macaulay helped out by sewing the stenciled curtains and painted pillows.

creating courage

Most kids seem to know, as I did, that they contain a very special life force. They have the power to imagine or visualize what it is they desire—from Shetland ponies to a land that is safe, protected and free—and then bring it into reality through the ideas and actions of the Creator within them. Spiritual wholeness is our natural state of being. We are all born believing, and creativity flows through us. Every young heart beats out a two-word prayer, *Create . . . believe . . . create . . . believe . . . create . . . believe . . . create . . . .*

Children intuitively understand that in order to feel better, they must take action. You may remember the story of the nine-year-old girl who was a war refugee in Kosovo. She had lost contact with her entire family, and to cope, she began to sing. She added verses daily, recalling good memories of her family. Anne Frank wrote in her diary as she hid from her Nazi oppressors. Noah, a young boy from Africa, carved a wooden bead for every day he lived through one of his continent's desperate famines. Struggling to process acts of terrorism, schoolchildren draw pictures. One girl drew a poetic image of the twin towers weeping. Some kids take creative community actions by making sandwiches for volunteer workers and collecting money. Other children envision our world as safe and free through stories they create together in group therapy.

In the Habitat for Humanity House of Belief workshops I founded, kids and adults alike become empowered to use their creativity to change their circumstances. As houses are transformed, hearts are transformed. When we see the power of our own positive ideas, and that our hands can "make" them real, our courage increases. We begin to believe that we can buy or build our own homes; or get a college degree; or open our own business; or even found a community program. One Habitat homeowner put it this way:

It is really important for me to set a good example for my children—to show them that mom can make what she needs for life and that they can too. I want them to believe that they have what they need inside of them. Money can't buy you satisfaction—that comes from yourself.

Kids' Sacred Places will help you to do just that: show your child that the courage we need comes from within, and is strengthened by surrounding ourselves with evidence of it. By introducing simple heart and hands projects to your child, you present him or her with creative actions to help them express their positive intentions, their beliefs, values, goals, and dreams for life. When we make our homes into Houses of Belief, we become immersed in a chivalrous setting, guaranteed to inspire heroism. In the following story, you will see how one child used these creative activities to make his bedroom transformation into a hero's story.

henry takes a stand

Henry Spain Burns, age seven, wants to be a writer. What, other than a writer, could a boy named *Henry Spain Burns* be, anyway? When I met Henry, just before he entered first grade, his name appeared to be the most exceptional thing about him. By all measures he was an average twenty-first century American boy who liked toy cars, video games, his father's farm and chickens, as well as the two Labrador puppies his mother had given him for Christmas. Henry was very talkative and happy to bestow me with the breadth of what he knew, including scientific facts he had picked up while watching the Discovery Channel or A & E.

One favorite true story had to do with a family member who had been electrocuted while wearing a metal (conductive) wristwatch during a storm. It seemed to have a *Ripley's Believe It or Not!* appeal for him. But he was also very happy to provide me with information that could potentially save my life. The lesson: only wear plastic watches! Assuming the role of hero seemed to please him, Henry really liked to do good things. And stories about others who did good things seemed to reinvigorate his own convictions. He was particularly impressed by the movie classic *To Kill A Mockingbird* and was quite expansive in his discussion of the movie's lesson: to stand up for what you believe in and to treat all people fairly, regardless of their skin color.

A KINDNESS CLOCK: After defending a deaf girl in his school classroom, Henry made a clock that illustrates his message to the world, "Make time to be kind."

No other experience to date, however, had made a greater impression upon the character of his spirit than the noble story of how Henry Spain Burns intervened on behalf of a student in his class. The other kids had been cruelly taunting Katie, a deaf girl who called upon sign language to supplement her own nonconventional style of speech. Another girl, Sarah, was particularly mean—often mimicking Katie's speech patterns and hands as she moved them to sign.

Like another great Henry—Shakespeare's Henry V on St. Crispin's Day—he stood up and gave a rousing speech, aimed at Katie's defense and the liberation of her spirit from her young oppressors. Here's what he said:

Just because people are different it doesn't mean they are bad—it actually means they are a little more special than us. In fact, we are just plain. We talk in easy ways; they have God's special gift language. You should never make fun of anyone. Just be kind.

When I asked Henry why people make fun of others, he replied, "That's been my question for a long time." All seven years of his life maybe? No doubt this conviction was reinforced by Henry's recent exposure to the heroic character, Scout, the little protagonist of *To Kill a Mockingbird*. She also did a good deed by seeing Boo as good, regardless of the evil threat rumors made him out to be. The retelling of this story became a regular event for Henry and one of the formative moments of his life so far. So much so, he even sought to immortalize his heroism in a short story, which we wrote together in his own *Book of Belief.*

getting started: make a book of belief

Whether you are age 7 or 37, the first step in making your home more meaningful is to take stock of what you care about: your beliefs, values, goals, dreams, memories, and best intentions. These positive ideas will become the inspiration for the decorating projects you express in creating a sacred place. You can catalog these uplifting concepts by making your own Book of Belief, or resource book. So, when it comes time to make something meaningful for your child's room, all you will need to do is reference the contents of your child's heart by referring to their Book of Belief.

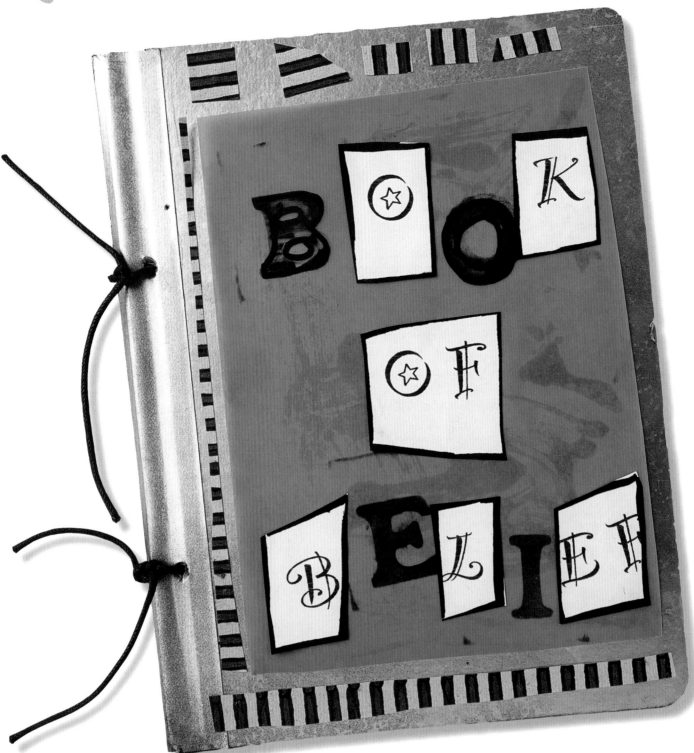

HEART AND HANDS PROJECT

heart objective: Have a meaningful discussion and sharing time, creating a list of the "heart concepts" of your child. The following questionnaire will help you. The answers to the questions will help you identify what is important and sacred to them. These will become the subjects for decorating their space. You can see how ideas from Henry's answers made their way into his Book of Belief sourcebook, and then into the things we created together.

hands activity: Using the questionnaire, we were able to look into the contents of Henry's heart. Then, we found or created words, pictures, or small objects to symbolize the things that are important to him. You can do this any way imaginable: hand written or drawn; cut from magazines or photographs; or even computer generated. The book itself may simply be a blank journal or a lined school-type of notebook.

BELIEF PAGES: Henry identified a belief about kindness to others and the value of trees and the environment.

HENRY'S BELIEF QUESTIONNAIRE

✳ *Your favorite colors and why?*

Bright, bright colors like orange, turquoise, and lime green because they are friendly like me.

Symbol: **Paint chips of the colors he chose.**

✳ *What makes you feel safe?*

My dogs, my home, and my mom and dad.

Symbol: **Photo of dogs and mom.**

✳ *Who do you look up to? Why?*

My dad is my hero, he knows a lot.

Symbol: **Dad's photo.**

✳ *What do people need to know about that you could tell them?*

I would tell them about wearing metal wristwatches in a storm—that you could get electrocuted.

✳ *What is your favorite thing to do?*

I like to make things, play with my dogs, and ride my bike. Also, I like taking care of the chickens at my dad's farm.

Symbol: **Hand-drawn chickens and dogs and a cut-out magazine picture of a bike.**

✳ *What would you like to be when you grow up?*

A writer, like Charles Dickens.

Symbol: **Picture of Charles Dickens and a pencil.**

✳ *What is your favorite book or movie? Why?*

TO KILL A MOCKINGBIRD, because Scout helps someone to be treated fairly.

Symbol: **Pictures of people of other colors.**

✳ *If you could change the world what would you do?*

Make everyone be kind and accept each other's differences.

Symbol: **Here, Henry wrote his story about the school incident in which he defended his deaf friend. The symbol was a hand to represent her sign language.**

seeing is believing

You may be thinking, "Just how does all of this translate into room dècor?" These meaningful heart concepts became the inspiration for nearly every element that Henry and I, his mom Stephanie, and our artist friend Jackie Denning handmade for his bedroom. We invented ways to incorporate the answers from his questionnaire into decorating projects for his room. With your child, look at Henry's answers and then try matching them to the item or area that was made to represent it. Henry's bedroom became a live-in version of his Book of Belief. It is an outward physical version of the inner contents of his young spirit—a fully illustrated "book of me." Through it, Henry says, "Here is what I look like inside, how I feel, what I believe in, and the dreams I hold dear."

Since Henry is my grandson (through marriage), we have spent our creative time together in spurts—like most families. Working around football and baseball practice and his parents' work schedules has provided what I call "growing time." As you know, kids change daily: one day they are enraptured with a particular space movie, proclaiming a career as an astronaut; a week later, they are on to something else. Over the last two years, Henry, has changed a lot. He now prefers to be called "Hank."

And does his room always look like the photos you see here? Of course not! It is always in flux, with his dirty clothes most often decorating the floor—to the frustration of his mom. (I know you can relate to this.) Our children require us to get over our need for the illusion of control. How can you control a small universe in the making? Even though it sometimes looks more like a cosmic explosion than an intentional world of Henry's own creation, it is his own world—a world that spins on one particular idea. Here is how Henry phrases it:

Whatever I think or believe in or choose to be or do is up to me. I am responsible for my life. In my bedroom I make stuff about these things—to remind me of what I am thinking. And like you say (Kelee), when you look at it or see it you believe in it.

The heart and hands projects that you see in Henry's room came into being over a two-year period. But even with the completion of just one, I could see Henry's self-worth growing. If you only have time to do just one of these meaningful activities, your child will benefit greatly. Each of these projects is easy to do and have been adapted for your use. First, answer the questionnaire above and make a Book of Belief, which will be your child's resource book. If necessary, do only one question a day for a week or more. Try to limit your creative time to your child's attention span: usually somewhere between 20 minutes and two hours. It is important to stop before everyone is worn out. Only you can gauge how much time you should spend.

As I mentioned in the introduction, when we surround our children with images that state something positive about them, they can more easily believe in themselves and their world. As Henry reminded us: *seeing is believing.* When you spend creative time together, your child's personal space becomes a visual affirmation that they are special, creative, and loved.

PERSONAL RESPONSIBILITY: Henry says "I am responsible for my life . . .whatever I think . . .or chose to do is up to me."

MAKE A SAFE-IN-BEDSPREAD: Using acrylic paint, an image is stenciled onto a sheet or bedspread. Henry's spread combines dog and bone images. Henry paints a foam-core headboard with a picture of his dog Phoebe.

make a "safe-in-bed" spread

When asked, Where do you feel safe? most kids say that being at home with mom and dad makes them feel best. Henry added his dogs Guinness and Phoebe to his safety equation. A *Safe-in-Bedspread* is a spin on the traditional "security blanket." This version allows a child to be involved in the creation of his/her own sense of safety. Henry drew pictures of his dogs, and then the pictures were used as patterns for creating a stencil or screen print to apply to his bedspread. A matching headboard was created from foam-core board.

HEART AND HANDS PROJECT

heart objective: To establish feelings of security, safety, and comfort at night.

hands activity: To paint, screen print, or stencil a bedspread with symbols of people, places, or things that make you or your child feel safe. Or make a foam-core headboard with your child's favorite symbol of safety, like Henry's headboard featuring his dog Phoebe.

steps to take: Detailed instructions found under the Safe-in-Bedspread photos.

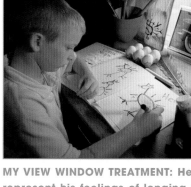

MY VIEW WINDOW TREATMENT: Henry, whose parents are divorced, drew chickens in his Book of Belief to represent his feelings of longing for his father and their farm. A stencil was made from the drawing and then applied to the curtains.

"my view" window treatment

A window provides a view out into the world. A *My View Window* Treatment—curtains, shades, or valance—is illustrated with colors and patterns that show a child's favored or most valued view of the world. Because Henry's parents are divorced, he can't always be at one of his favorite places: his father's farm. So, we chose to embellish Henry's curtain and window shade with the chickens, barn, and dog bones you might find there.

HEART AND HANDS PROJECT

heart objective: To provide uplifting images that encourage a child to keep their values in view.

hands activity: To paint, apply with felt, stamp, screen print, or stencil uplifting and valued images to a window treatment.

steps to take: Detailed instructions found under the My View Window Treatment photos.

A MAKING TIME CLOCK: Make symbols that represent the theme or message for your clock. Apply them to the canvas board with paint, paste or any other materials you like. Install the clock parts per the manufacturer's simple instructions.

paint a "making time" clock

We all want more time to do the things we love and need reminders of what we intend to do more often. Kids sometimes feel like the adults in their lives don't spend enough time with them. A *Making Time Clock* offers a great opportunity to have a meaningful conversation together about what we believe in. Henry focused on a positive belief that he has: *"That we must all take more time to be kind,"* like he did when he defended his deaf classmate. When illustrated with words or pictures, the clock serves as a reminder of our child's good intentions.

HEART AND HANDS PROJECT

heart objective: To acknowledge our beliefs and create a visual reminder of our intention to act on them.

hands activity: Using a canvas board and simple clock kit, paint or collage a clock to represent the desired activities.

steps to take: Detailed instructions found under the Making Time Clock photos.

CREATE A COMFORT CUSHION: With a permanent magic marker on a self-made or ready-made smooth cotton pillow, draw a picture of the person, place or thing that brings you or your child comfort. Then, use acrylic or fabric paints to color in the image. Jackie Denning helped comfort Henry by bringing his dad into view.

create a "comfort cushion"

When parents are not together, because of separation or divorce, kids can become lonely for the missing parent. It's even harder, of course, for children who have actually lost a parent in life. Just having a physical representation of that parent close by can be comforting. A soft pillow with their likeness on it—for holding and squeezing—is even better. Try the *Comfort Cushion* project for absent grandparents, siblings, and friends, too. Henry's pillow represents his dad.

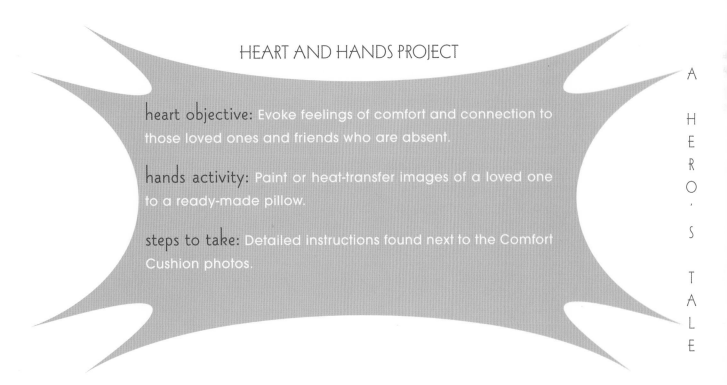

HEART AND HANDS PROJECT

heart objective: Evoke feelings of comfort and connection to those loved ones and friends who are absent.

hands activity: Paint or heat-transfer images of a loved one to a ready-made pillow.

steps to take: Detailed instructions found next to the Comfort Cushion photos.

CHAPTER 3

a place of belonging

Henry's room is definitely a place of *belonging* just like mine was at his age. And Henry himself is a whole and capable vessel—that magical beret-wearing, paintbrush-wielding ginger jar come to life. His bedroom is a happy and safe studio of our creation where acts of courage come easy, even for fragile jars like us that can be so easily broken.

If we are created as precious and rare vessels, then the safe haven of our parents' home can be like a guarded pedestal in a national museum. Preserving belief and creativity is much easier there than anywhere else—even much more so than at school. Every parent dreads the day that a negative outside experience will leave the first small fissure in our child's vessel of belief and creativity. We would do anything to prevent it. But we know it will come, just as it did for us when we were small. It could originate in mean words from playground antagonists that say: we are too big, our clothing isn't right, or our skin is the wrong color. These personal attacks diminish self-esteem and confidence.

VISUAL AFFIRMATIONS: Jessica created an area in her room that models her dream of becoming a marine biologist. Shaking off unkindness she encountered at school, the 13-year-old redirected her thoughts by painting an undersea mural and creating a marine research station.

Kids' Sacred Places will give you the tools and inspiration you need to keep that young vessel intact. Even when small cracks appear, the healing and renewing creative process of this book will help you to do the mending. The following chapters will uplift and support you in preserving your young vessel by creating belief-filled environments.

The next inspiring story will even provide some help for big kids who may need a little mending themselves. Many adults in my workshops share stories about experiences in childhood that they feel are holding them back from their true potential and highest purpose. Such limiting concepts can originate on the playground or in the classroom. Or, they can just as easily be the result of water cooler gossip at work or family issues like divorce. Any of these can make us feel "broken," like a ginger jar that has suffered a fall.

the broken vessel

Broken to bits. That's how the Berkovich family felt. Jodi and Al had just come together through remarriage, happily sweeping together their individual pieces—four children, two each—into one big pile. Still, they were far from being a work of art. Jodi described it this way:

> *Our family was like a puzzle—or a mosaic table—with pieces missing. Though we wanted to put it together we felt we didn't have all that we needed to do so. We were constantly struggling to find ways for the kids in our new family to get along. All of the kids, except little Alex, were still angry at us for getting divorced from their other parents. Anna and Alexis, who were close to the same age, were competitive and envious; they fought so much they nearly drove all of us apart. Jessica, at age 13, was going through the transition from little girl to teenager. And Alex was having trouble with school bullies. My new husband and I, though very much in love, felt very guilty at the same time.*

Jodi and Al are representative of many blended families who at first only seem to have one thing in common: their shared pain. Over the last four years, I have worked with the Berkovich family intensively, helping them to think and act creatively, calling upon heart and hands projects to help them to heal their relationships and make their home a sacred reflection of those changes. This creative family has been kind enough to invite us into their place

A FAMILY MOSAIC: This blended family overcame their differences by bringing their "broken pieces" together into a healing mosaic. Through this proactive step they were able to see themselves as "whole" again.

of belief and belonging. In coming chapters, we will enter the bedrooms of each of their children. What you will witness is a *visual affirmation* of what is possible when the spirit of creativity flows through our hearts, hands, homes, and families. And since seeing is believing, you will begin to believe that it is also possible for your own family.

In the days before television and mass production, family creativity was the norm, not the exception. Creativity was not only a means of making what you needed to live—food, clothing, furniture, and even the house itself—but also of family sharing and entertainment. Think back to the Victorian-era book, *Little Women* by Louisa May Alcott, or rent the movie and watch it with the kids. It paints a sentimental picture of joyful family times filled with music, drama, art, and games. Also, it illustrates an era of more clearly outlined family values. Modern cynicism may tempt us to dismiss such an idealistic world. However, it would be tragic to overlook the valuable reminder Alcott's story contains: family creative activities can help us to relate to each other once again.

FAMILY VALUES: The Berkovichs, a blended family, identified what they share in common and illustrated their beliefs, values, goals, and dreams in their family Book of Belief.

In our time, families need all the help they can get in the areas of bonding and communication. The statistics predict that nearly half of all marriages will end in divorce; and second marriages that blend children together are even more at risk. The challenge of co-parenting with former spouses is fraught with the potential for adult conflicts, conflicts that are sometimes insurmountable. All the more reason to equip ourselves and our children with heart and hand techniques that can help us to learn, heal, and grow many times over. This creative process can provide us with coping skills for a lifetime; helping us to survive—no matter what may come our way. In gathering together the lost pieces, whether due to divorce or any other kind of personal or family brokenness, it is best to begin by looking for what is good in our lives.

missing pieces

I asked the Berkovich family to begin by focusing on the positive concepts they share: their individual and mutual beliefs, values, goals, and dreams for life. They started by making lists together. Then I asked them to create an illustrated book of their answers. I call this heart and hands project a family Book of Belief. In the last chapter, Henry made a similar book about his own intentions for life. The idea is to use pictures, words, symbols, drawings, photos, or small objects to represent their shared ideas. Identifying these important family beliefs and values is like finding the missing pieces to the mosaic puzzle.

The Berkovichs' BELIEFS:

- We believe in God.
- We believe in fairness and equality.
- We believe in helping the environment.
- We believe we can do anything together.
- We believe in the power of love.

VALUES:

- We value each other.
- We value actions of kindness.
- We value peaceful communication.
- We value hugs.

GOALS:

- We want to help others.
- We want to recycle.
- We want to organize a community food drive.
- We want to improve our home.

DREAMS:

- We dream of traveling throughout the world.
- We dream of living by the ocean.
- We dream of a Disneyworld vacation.
- We dream of becoming athletes and scholars.

COMMUNITY VALUES:

- We value our teachers.
- We value our friends.
- We value a good school.
- We value stay-at-home parents.

book of belief pages: beliefs, values, goals, & dreams

Take this opportunity to make your own lists, just like Jodi and Al's family. Add the ideas to your Book of Belief. Then, start thinking of pictures, signs, symbols, or drawings that will illustrate each statement. These will come in handy when you begin to create your own sacred places. These intentions will serve as inspiration for the heart and hands projects that you create. The Berkovichs incorporated their intentions into a mosaic table.

The Book of Belief they created helped them to identify what was important to each member of the family. With such a validation, who wouldn't feel as if they belonged? To further give form to their newly-shared vision, I suggested that the family literally create a mosaic table to celebrate the recovery of their lost or broken fragments. They would organize them into a unified whole, making a perfect symbol of the new family all together: a living work of art.

These two heart and hands projects, the Book of Belief and a *Mosaic of Life* are easy to accomplish. The Book of Belief will give you essential information for making your entire home a sacred place of belief and belonging. And the mosaic will be a constant visual reminder of all that is positive, even in times of heartache.

making a "mosaic of life"

Sometimes our lives can feel broken. All of the good things seem to have gone to pieces. That's how the Berkovich family felt just after remarriage had made them into a new "blended" family. To identify what they shared and to celebrate their "wholeness" and unity as a family, they created a mosaic table. As they put the pieces back together again, they envisioned their shared values. They represented these ideas in their design: a heart represents their parents' love, a stone wall reminds them never to create barriers of communication, a stream of water says "go with the flow," friendship blooms in flower motifs, family growth is green grass, and the sun shines for peace and harmony.

MAKING A MEANINGFUL MOSAIC: Using smooth-edged mosaic pieces or broken tiles that have been made child-safe, use tile adhesive to fix them to a table-top or other surface. When the adhesive has set (about 24 hours) work the grout into the crevices (see manufacturer's instructions).

HEART AND HANDS PROJECT

heart objective: To identify our broken or lost positive intentions for life, then to bring them together in a vision of wholeness.

hands activity: Label each broken tile or mosaic piece with an intention. Place it into the artwork.

steps to take: Detailed instructions found under Meaningful Mosaic photos.

MENDING BROKENNESS: The finished mosaic represents the new family's heart intentions of love, friendship, travel, and growth.

heartache? then handmake

Jessica Collins, 13, is the oldest of Jodi and Al Berkovich's blended family. And throughout one particular school year, her tender heart was always aching. Tall for her age, big boned, and of healthy weight (just like I was), she was the brunt of terrible remarks (just like I was). During the most vulnerable time in a young girl's life, early adolescence, when dad takes backseat to the attention of boys at school, Mickey Mouse gets replaced by MTV icons, and unrealistic standards of beauty leap off every magazine cover, Jessica found herself displaced and alone. Her self-esteem was plummeting:

> *Sometimes people won't even give you a chance to be their friend because of how big you are. They look on the outside and not the inside. The gossip and unkindness that gets passed through three-way phone calls and e-mails really hurts. It kills a person very quickly. You feel like you are dying inside.*

Remembering our success with the family's first creative projects together, Jodi asked me for further help. Thinking back to my own past, to a time when I had many personal negatives to release, I remembered a very special chair. The gist of it is, that chair project helped to save my life. It allowed me to purge all the negative things I had come to believe about myself, such as ideas I had absorbed at school, in my family, through religion, and in mass culture. I knew a "chair healing" could help Jessica too. But first, we needed a little more *positive* information.

Jodi noted that in their family Book of Belief Jessica had declared her goal and dream for life: to become a marine biologist. I suggested that our goal be to help Jessica make her bedroom a representation of her dream, keeping her surrounded with positive reminders of who she really is, what she believes in, and what she dreams of becoming. It would be the ultimate place of belonging, like living inside of her own personal Book of Belief.

As we discussed a plan with Jessica, some of Jodi's own fears and negative thoughts came up:

I just felt incapable of really doing this with her. One of the ideas was for an undersea mural. I had no art experience. To do something like that you have to be trained or skilled. My life has been as a suburban wife with a day-job at an energy company. In magazines, I see designers and decorators doing those things. You are supposed to have someone do it for you. I have no art background. I was really afraid. But my daughter's self-esteem was at stake. So, somehow I knew I must try.

Jodi was suffering from what I call *masterpiece anxiety;* this happens when we put too much pressure on ourselves, based on our worn-out beliefs. Like those created by negative experiences in school art classes, the inability to do the required drawings and formal assignments leave some believing they are not creative or "artistic." There are others who can draw a perfect still life with their eyes closed. There appear to be only a few real artists or performers or designers—those who exhibit in galleries or perform in concerts or design homes for the rich and famous.

I suggested that Jessica *and* Jodi each do a "chair healing" project to get them started. In this project, we are able to let go of negative thoughts and feelings of inadequacy, replacing them with positive affirmations. First, the negatives are written on the fabric of the old and dirty chair (curbside discards work well for this). Then we tear away the fabric—shredding it—thereby removing our old ideas as well. Finally, positive words, symbols, and colors are applied to the chair as it is re-upholstered. The chair is transformed and so are our beliefs. The *Re-Upholstering Me* project allowed Jessica and her mom Jodi to know they have the creative power of change within them. Their motto: "Heartache? Then handmake!"

Jodi added:

It felt so good to write down all of those negatives and then shred the fabric. It really helped me to let go of those negative beliefs. It gave me a fresh start. I have been able to become aware of my own creativity and my daughters' rooms are a testimony of how we have grown.

Today, Jessica's bedroom is a perfect example of how to live inside your dream. She has learned the process of *make* and then believe:

HEARTACHE? THEN HANDMAKE! Jessica writes positive sayings on a freshly-decorated chair for her room.

When I make something for my room, it gives me the power to believe that I can do anything. I was just accepted into a great school that will help me academically to keep pursuing my dream of becoming a marine biologist. And I just returned from a special studies dolphin camp where I actually got to swim with them!

Jessica gives us valuable advice on how to become friends with people and not judge them on their appearance. You'd think she were diving into the ocean to greet a dolphin:

It is simple. Close your eyes. Hold your nose. And just start talking.

"re-upholstering" me

RE-UPHOLSTERING ME: Jodi Berkovich, 35, follows her daughter's lead and lets go of her own negative and limiting feelings in a heart and hands project.

In this exercise, Jodi, who had no formal art training, wanted to help her daughter with creative decorating for her bedroom but had doubts of her own ability. She felt that perhaps she wasn't qualified enough to even try to be creative. Jessica and Jodi had both had some negative experiences that were hard to forget. Both mother and daughter learned that changing negative thoughts to positive ones could be as easy as fixing up a worn-out chair.

HEART AND HANDS PROJECT

heart objective: Transforming negative experiences and thoughts to positive affirmations.

hands activity: Do a "me" furniture fix-up. Go to a thrift store, yard sale, or other venue for old, inexpensive furniture. Finding cast-off furniture on the street can be especially symbolic. Find chairs that look like each of you feels inside, perhaps worn and a little beat up.

steps to take: Using a marker pen, ask your child to write directly on the chair fabric (or wood) the hurtful words or experiences he or she would like to obliterate. When finished, pull off the fabric and tear or cut it to shreds, allowing the negative feelings to be destroyed with the old, dirty fabric. Repeat the process for yourself.

Now create a vibrant new plan for the chair. Repaint and upholster it with colors and designs that represent the positive beliefs that you wish to celebrate. Finish by writing uplifting words and phrases on the new re-upholstered chair. Have your child visualize the fresh, new chair as themselves.

MAKING SELF-ESTEEM: Jessica created a vibrant new plan for a chair. She repaired it with colors and designs that represent her positive beliefs. The affirmation chair symbolizes her ability to hand-make her own self-esteem.

build a "dream box"

For as long as she can remember, Jessica has loved the ocean, especially dolphins. This interest has led to a dream of one day becoming a marine biologist. She envisions herself in a research station by the ocean, close enough to hear the dolphins talk. To help her believe in her dream even more, she has decided she would like to live inside of it and make her room into a representation of her underwater and seaside workplace. But first she must make a plan—a small and yet sacred model of what she would like her room to be about—a *Dream Box.*

HEART AND HANDS PROJECT

heart objective: To empower personal belief and a vision for the attainment of goals and dreams and to build confidence in planning and creative skills.

hands activity: Using a small shoebox or wood shadow box, create a model of your goal or dream. Use any materials you can think of. Try to avoid buying prefabricated miniatures. It will be more fun and rewarding to make your own.

A DREAM BOX: This shadow box, or "Dream Box", represents Jessica's dream of a seaside career.

paint a "dreamscape"

Think of the land or place of your child's dreams. Could it be in a cabin deep in the forest, behind a desk at *The New York Times,* or on the plains of the Serengeti? What do they dream of becoming in life? Where do they dream of going? One good way to keep our dreams in view is by painting a mural big enough to surround us with that dream. Refer to your Dream Box. Enlarge a portion of the scene you created or create another. Research your dream location. Go to the library and check out books that can help you create your scene. Movies can help you visualize in 3-D. Jessica painted her dream of being under the sea. If you need help, ask an artist, like Jackie Denning, to help you draw the scene with a black marker. Then you and your child can paint it in living color. Asking friends and other family members to participate makes for creative bonding.

PAINT A DREAMSCAPE: Using black acrylic paint or a magic marker draw symbols or scenes to represent your child's goals or dreams. Free hand or trace your ideas onto canvas or paper. Artist Jackie Denning helped Jodi and Jessica get started by drawing an underwater scene for them on canvas. Parents remember, you may include as many creative friends and family as you would like to help with these projects.

HEART AND HANDS PROJECT

heart objective: To help a young heart to live inside their dreams for life and to believe that they are possible.

hands activity: On canvas, first draw and then paint in the dream destination.

steps to take: Detailed instructions found under Dreamscape photo.

DREAMSCAPE: Once they started, all fears about trying an art project were literally "painted away." The two painted Jessica's dream into reality. And, they had fun doing it!

LISTENED   THANKED   HELPED

Forgave

BELIEVED

SHARED

CHAPTER 4

flowers that empower

I have never read or heard of a story in which there are two princesses who share their reign equally. In fairy tales, and even in recorded history, when there are two princes, or even brothers, they are always battling, attempting to do away with the other. The Bible story of Cain and Abel is the classic example of sibling rivalry. But traditionally, our authors have been much less explicit about the archetypal relationship of sisters in literature and history.

However, we do repeatedly see much competition amongst storybook women. Consider the tale of Snow White. When her father married her stepmother, the new queen set out to poison her. She chanted, "Mirror, mirror, on the wall, who's the fairest of them all?" Obviously threatened by Snow White's purity and goodness, and not wanting to share her husband with his beautiful daughter, the queen plotted against her. And of course Cinderella is just another variation on the same theme, this time, with the stepmother *and* stepsisters joining together to persecute her.

FLOWER EMPOWERING WALLS: Two warring step-sisters learned to share a bedroom and became good friends by using Gerber Daisies as a positive symbol.

When Alexis, age 11, and Anna, age 9, became sisters through remarriage, there was no less scheming involved. Prior to the new marriage, they had each held the coveted position of youngest in their families and were privileged with many advantages. Each a "daddy's little girl," their places were established and without threat. Alexis noted that suddenly their roles were challenged:

> *I just didn't know what was going to happen, because I didn't really fit in any longer. Al, my new step-dad, just seemed to be so big and tough, yet he was so giving to Anna. I missed my own dad. I wanted to have my friends over, so I would have someone on my side. One time when we each had friends over, it was like two gangs against the other. My friends were really picking on Anna. I started to feel sorry for her then.*

Jodi, Alexis's mom, says that the competition was so intense they had to ban groups of their friends from coming over:

> *We just wanted the girls to learn to relate to each other, independent of their friends. They needed to become friends on their own. It wasn't unusual to hear "I hate you!" coming from their bedroom. We were all driven apart by their warring. It was compounded by the fact that our house is so small they had to share a room together. One of their tendencies was to count, divide, and quarter everything that was given to them, each making sure they got their share. They were so jealous and "snotty" to each other. We would have to cancel family events because of them.*

When the parents and I began to work with the two girls, it was established that their bedroom-decorating project would happen as a result of their commitment to healing their relationship. In other words, without kindness, sharing, and cooperation, there would be no decorating. The girls reluctantly agreed to participate. Also, Jodi and Al laid down the law, and applied both love and logic. The girls would choose their actions, and therefore, the positive or negative outcome. To reward kindness, they would be able to beautify their room through the creative projects we planned. If they chose to remain hostile, their room would remain as barren and ugly as their relationship had become.

LOVE AND LOGIC: Alexis and Anna's room is a visual affirmation of the fun and friendship they found through heart and hand decorating. The dark basement bedroom was as transformed as their relationship.

love and logic

This cause-and-effect methodology is one that is highly acclaimed and taught by a parenting resource group called The Love and Logic Institute. The love aspect allows a child to grow through their mistakes. Logic allows them to live with the consequences of their choices. Jim Fay, Bob Sornson, and Foster Cline, co-authors of *Meeting the Challenge, Using Love and Logic to Help Children Develop Attention and Behavior Skills*, offer three simple rules:

- Give choices within limits
- Set limits through enforceable statements
- Apply consequences without anger

Fay, a former teacher and school principal, elaborates:

I tell parents I can change their lives by teaching them two things. The first is that parents have a job setting limits. The other is that kids have a job testing those limits.

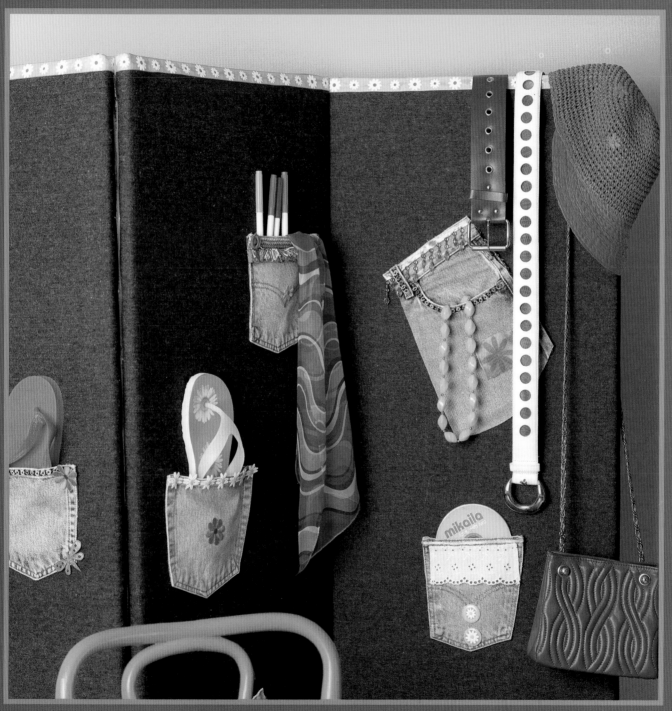

A SACRED BLUE JEAN SCREEN: This room divider honors the girls' individual spaces within the shared room.

This is precisely what was happening in the Berkovich household. Jodi and Al had to be diligent in enforcing their rules. At last, the girls were given two weeks to shape-up. As we started our project, the parents and I committed to being consistently fair. We listened to Anna's and Alexis's ideas and preferences with equal interest. The first group discussion about their room was a little rough, with the old competitiveness resurfacing. But it didn't take long for them to find out that they had more in common with each other than they thought. Anna described the process:

It was great because we each got to decide what we liked and got to feel involved. We wrote down our ideas and made lists of what we liked and what had meaning to us. And guess what? We liked the same things! So, we put our ideas together.

Alexis continued:

At first it was scary, but good. We liked real bright colors and flowers. Before, our dads and the boys in the family didn't like our choices. They didn't believe in us this way. Now, we have each other. Now, I have a friend who lives with me! It is sooooo cool.

Based on their love of brightly-colored daisies, we created a heart and hands project that would inspire them to take positive and loving actions toward one another. After painting their walls in yellow to represent Anna and purple for Alexis, we sketched out a pattern of Gerber Daisies with which to embellish them. The catch? One daisy would be added to the wall each time one of the girls made a loving gesture toward the other. Logic would inspire the girls to choose actions that would provide a beautiful outcome. The wall would represent their good actions, the flowers empowering their relationship to heal and grow.

Anna, 9, and Alexis, 11, added one Gerber Daisy to their wall for every kind word or action toward one another. Alexis uses hot glue to apply a flower and Anna writes its meaning in chalk.

sacred objects

Ryan, a seven-year-old, fair-haired little boy, like a prince from a Celtic legend, lives a few doors down from me. The other day he showed me his treasure. In a cigar box, which was given to him by his mom, Bridget, he has many special objects. Foremost is a very old saltwater compass passed down to him through his father from his grandfather. There are also rocks, leaves, and twigs, all found in mysterious places; one of his baby teeth; a "neat-o" combination fan and cutting tool from Cub Scout camp; candy sprinkles, for courage when he needs it; a Pokemon gold dragon; and a roll of masking tape. Ryan discusses these objects with the gravity of one in the possession of a "sacred cache":

> These are my really important things. This compass was from World War II; my grandfather was a hero on a submarine. My dad's gone mostly now since the divorce and my compass makes me think of him. I like this tape I have, too. It makes it so that I can fix stuff. I could fix just about anything with this tape. And this dragon protects me at night when I have bad dreams.

Whether in a cigar box, beneath a mattress, or in a blue jean pocket, kids easily attach profound and magical meanings to special objects: a bird's wing found the day your grandfather died; an earring pulled from the lake by a fishing hook; your first ribbon from the science fair; or your kitten's ball of yarn. These relics can rouse lost feelings, and help us to remember something we have forgotten. Personally, I have been a life-long keeper of these mysteries from childhood embedded in feather and enamel. This fascination with how time, experience, and perception gets caught in material forms has led me to shape my home into a life-sized cigar box filled with sacred objects. Somehow, I have retained my facility with this childhood language, bringing shape and form to invisible, spiritual concepts. For example, the bird's wing means that my grandfather has taken flight; the earring was, of course, lost by a mermaid with red hair like mine; the science ribbon reminds me that I am capable of genius; and the kitten's yarn tells of how much I loved her.

Undoubtedly for Anna and Alexis, a Gerber Daisy will always mean *I have a sister and friend.* The girls describe their relationship now:

A CREATIVE MIRACLE: Step-sisters, who at one time barely spoke, now love to share time together reading out loud. This whimsical bookkeeper pillow was created from an old pair of blue jeans.

LITTLE HOUSE
Laura Ingalls Wilder

LAURA INGALLS WILDER

Little House
on the Prairie

We are great friends. We love to read to each other. Our favorites are Little House on the Prairie, Junie B. Jones, *and* Hitty: Her First Hundred Years. *We also do things for each other . . . like pick each other's clothes up and remind each other about homework.*

Miraculous! Pick up each other's clothes? Hard enough to get one to do it, let alone for each other. You are probably thinking we have crossed back over into the fairytale world. But their mom, Jodi, confirms that it is true:

Our home is so much calmer, happier, and in harmony now. We don't have to resolve many issues with them. They resolve them themselves.

Alexis and Anna—a picture is worth a million words.

So, for all of us who were involved in planting this empowering garden, the Gerber Daisy will always be a sacred symbol of healing. (Interesting, because so many holistic remedies can be found in flowers and plants.) Remember that what is perceived as sacred is different for each of us. We each choose to invest our belief in a symbol that is personally relevant. The daisies became representative of the changes that the girls chose to make in their lives. What changes would you like your child to make? Or, what changes would your child like to make for him/herself? The following questionnaire will help you assess the growth opportunities that are possible for our kids, and even ourselves, by applying the love and logic principles in creating a sacred place. In preparing to plant—or hot glue—*flowers that empower,* we must begin by sowing seeds of good thoughts and pulling any weedy ones.

NURTURING THE SEEDS

&

WEEDING THE GARDEN

✻ Are you kind to yourself? If not, what would you like to change?

✻ What good things do you believe or say about yourself? What would you like to be able to believe/say about yourself? Why?

✻ Do you get along with others? At school? In your family? If so, why? If not, why? What would you do, if you could, to change the situation?

✻ Do you think about good things? What are they?

✻ Are there things you have a hard time accepting about people you know? What are they?

✻ When people upset or hurt you, how do you get over it? Can you forgive them?

✻ Describe the ideal you. Who would you be if you could? What do you look and act like? How do you treat people? What do you think about yourself?

Now, choose one of the changes you and your child would like to encourage. For example, Brandon has feelings of low self-esteem and is plagued by negative thoughts. Ashley has trouble finishing her homework. Cami's room is always a mess, and she expects her mom to clean it. Josh watches television nonstop and rarely talks to his family. Annette gossips at school and has few friends. James brings his *Gameboy* to the dinner table and everywhere else!

The general concept of the *Flower Empower Wall* can be adapted to suit your child's own age and interests. Brandon can use a rubber stamp to add a soccer ball symbol to his wall every time he has a positive thought about himself. Ashley, who likes to make beaded jewelry, can add a designated number of beads to a lampshade each time she completes her homework. Cami, who wants to be a fashion designer and is really into color, may paint a section of her room, for each week it stays orderly. Or, of course, you can employ the following heart and hands project, just like Anna and Alexis.

book of belief: add your own sacred symbols

Together with your child, decide on your own sacred symbols. Choose one to represent the change you would both like to make and add it to a page in your Book of Belief. Look around your child's bedroom for clues as to what might be sacred to them. Is there a treasure box or even a photo album? (Be sure and do this with their approval—privacy should be respected.) What positive objects or experiences are represented there? Remember, Anna and Alexis used the Gerber Daisy to represent sharing and kindness. Brandon chose the soccer ball to represent positive thoughts. Ashley utilized beads to reward her self-discipline. Cami chose four colors, one for each wall she got to paint. The colors represented her respect for her mom, her self-reliance, her dream to be a designer, and neatness.

flower for "your good thoughts"
wall, lamp, or pillow

Anna and Alexis just couldn't get along. They were competitive and jealous, *and* they also had to share a bedroom. Here is how we used love and logic to create a decorating project that would grow out of their forgiving and kind actions. The same process will encourage any child to make the logical choice: creativity over conflict.

A FLOWER FOR YOUR GOOD THOUGHTS WALL, LAMP, OR PILLOW: Using a low temperature hot glue gun or tacky glue, apply silk flowers to pillows, lampshades, or walls.

HEART AND HANDS PROJECT

heart objective: To encourage positive and loving actions between siblings or toward the child him/herself.

hands activity: Create a flower wall in which every flower represents a positive word or deed by the kids toward each other. Hence, the beautiful wall is created by their good intentions or actions. If your child wants—using chalk—label the flower with the thought or action it represents. The same process may be used to create the daisy pillow or lampshade.

steps to take: Detailed instructions found under Your Good Thoughts Wall, Lamp, or Pillow photo.

a "sacred blue jeans" screen & pillow

Blue jeans pockets rank right up there with cigar boxes and tree houses as sacred holding places for kids' treasured stuff. Marbles, frogs, buttons, gum (chewed or fresh), rocks, books, and baseball cards are just some of the coveted objects to be found there. Alexis and Anna needed a little privacy and a place for each to store their prized possessions; so they created a *Sacred Blue Jeans Screen*. Blue denim and recycled jeans pockets are the foundation of this room divider and pillow.

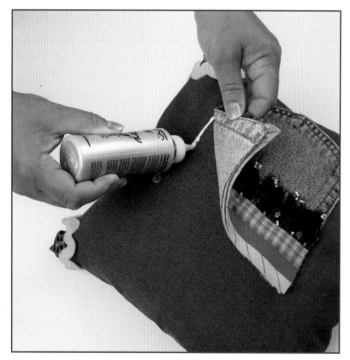
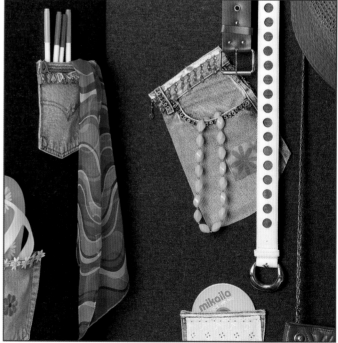

A SACRED BLUE JEANS SCREEN AND PILLOW: Make a screen from a wood frame and cover it with blue denim stapled into place. Pockets from old jeans can then be glued to the screen and pillow surface with tacky glue.

HEART AND HANDS PROJECT

heart objective: To give each girl a feeling of spatial privacy, and also to provide "secret compartments" for their special stuff.

hands activity: Cover a wood frame with denim and pockets. The kids will love applying their own embellishments like fringe, beads, lace, buttons, and more. The screen's not complete until the pockets have been thoughtfully filled with treasures.

steps to take: Detailed instructions found under Sacred Blue Jeans Screen and Pillow photos.

CHAPTER 5

becoming real again

You may remember the story of *The Velveteen Rabbit,* the little stuffed bunny who became real when he knew that his boy really loved him. That velvet bunny is symbolic of all of us. When we look at a small child, we know we are seeing the real thing. Like the bunny, an act of love has made them so. Babies welcome each new face with expectancy and an open heart. These little spirit houses of love haven't yet become interrupted by walls of rejection. There are no rooms for fear, hiding, or self-criticism. They are born believing in their freedom of personal expression and their right to unconditional acceptance. We wonder how anyone could have ever taken away our own right to be loved for who we are, licensing us to be truly real.

   Often, as adults we only feel safe to be ourselves—not our reserved workplace self, but the playful one who goes for the hat with the big orange Gerber Daisy on the brim—when no one is looking. When we were kids, we could have cared less if anyone was watching. Oh, but, if only the years could have kept that little pony-riding, jewelry-making, dancing girl intact—the kid with the canary yellow walls. My story, as I mentioned, was very much like Jessica's. And probably a lot like your own. It was fraught with adolescent experiences like

CELEBRATING TRUE COLORS: Rebeka, 15, gave her favorite colors special meanings—they represent her life values of faith, family, future, friends, and love.

peer pressure and family expectations that can make us become less than real. To survive we need to feel loved. Feeling like we are in a fight for our lives, we begin to be who it seems family and friends will love. This agreement that we make—to deny our real self in exchange for love—also has the media's seal of approval.

If you want to know the right way to look, act, dress, or even decorate your house, just consult a magazine or peruse the television commercials. Concepts about what is correct, socially acceptable, or beautiful are sold to us, convincing us that we must buy services and products to be lovable. *The Velveteen Rabbit* is sold plastic surgery for his oversized ears, a special conditioner for more manageable fur, and is told that he really should learn to control the twitch in his tail (when he feels joy it shakes uncontrollably). The hut in which he lives, friends say, seriously needs an interior decorator. He wonders, "Or, could I do the decorating myself?" Of course, the boy who truly loves him wouldn't have it any other way.

golden bunny huts

When it came to decorating her room, Jessica, our real-life Velveteen Rabbit, and the girl who loves her mom, Jodi, wouldn't have had it any other way either. But for Jodi it was hard to find the belief to begin the project. She is like so many parents who are still struggling to become real themselves, even while helping their children. Her feelings of inadequacy about her own creativity are very common.

It has become in vogue and safe for parents to hire someone else to "do the kid's room." Julie Iovine of *The New York Times* reports that parents are buying rare, museum-quality antiques for their decorators to install into their kids' rooms. In a story ominously titled, "For Kids' Rooms, Bunnies Are Out, Biedermeier Is In," she tells of a parent spending $8,000 for an antique spittoon to contain their child's marbles. Another considered a $35,000 bookcase. These examples may be extreme, but in suburbs across the country a milder form of designer spending is taking place. In my own neighborhood a chic little children's bedroom boutique charges as much as $1,500 for infant comforters and other equally pricey items.

CREATING CONFETTI: "Beka," as her friends call her, used squares of tissue paper to create her joyful confetti-strewn walls.

Don't get me wrong, there are times when a good holistic decorator or artisan can be of great assistance in helping you to liberate your creativity and ideas. In fact, I conduct workshops to train decorators and designers in *belief-based decorating*, empowering them to take a more meaningful approach in assisting their clients. However, the myth of interior design, as an area outside of what any child of the Creator could accomplish, has been a very profitable one in our consumer culture, requiring us to buy expensive and often meaningless material things to fill the emptiness of our hearts and houses. In the gilded cages—or rabbit huts—of fashion that we forge, our creative spirits have no key. We find our children and ourselves in a fight for our very lives—our spiritual lives. After all, once we have spent so much money and time getting the "style" right, how can we change it as we evolve and grow? Decorating our homes through such inauthentic means keeps us from who we really are and where our creative hearts compel us to go. Certainly, it can be equally as limiting for our children.

Many adults I have worked with in creating nurturing environments for themselves say that their most damaging experiences came from the words or actions of their own parents. Take my friend Diane, for example, who loved to make paper collages when she was a child. For her, it was a great way to communicate what she was feeling. She was born with a cleft palette, which made her self-conscious. She was shy and felt embarrassed about speaking. Her elementary school teachers said that her artwork, particularly the collages, were brilliant. She won several awards to prove it. But her parents never attended the special exhibits or open houses to honor the winners. And while other children's parents hung their artwork and homework in the kitchen and throughout the house, her parents did not. In fact, once her mom said it didn't match her new wallpaper. To Diane, it meant that her mother didn't place value on her creative talent. She felt that her mother's decorating and furniture were more important. As an adult, Diane has struggled to place value on her creativity, since the inadvertent message her mother conveyed through her neglect had demeaned it.

As the case of Diane illustrates, we simply must not put our own decorating schemes or plans over the creative expressions of our children. Our own creativity, like Diane's, may still be suffering from similar experiences. In preparation for a television show on which I was to appear, the producers shared letters from young viewers with me. The kids said they felt they didn't belong in their parents' houses because they couldn't get near the expensive furniture. School was hard enough with no sense of belonging because of peer pressure and

STAINED-GLASS FRIENDS: Colored Plexiglas embellished with images of Beka and her friends are linked together with key chain. This colorful window treatment helps keep Beka's cherished friendships in sight—and mind.

cliques, and their homes were not much better. They seemed to ask, "Shouldn't *I* be the object of such care and importance as the fancy decorating?"

If you find yourself struggling to release negative ideas and false beliefs about your own creative abilities, like Diane and Jodi, then you are not alone. When we know that we are unconditionally loved and supported in becoming real, we get the courage to wear that orange-flowered hat, even when everyone is looking.

Know that success is all about trying. Someone said that God only requires that you try, not succeed. Really, isn't success spending fun and meaningful time together anyway? Here is how one interior designer learned to break all the rules, skipping-out on the style rhetoric she had learned to live with in her profession, and rekindle her own playful creativity—all of this while helping her daughter to express the contents of her heart.

CULTURAL CUES: Subtle references to Beka's Korean heritage can also be found in her sacred place.

true colors

For Rebeka Brown, or "Beka" as her friends call her, each color in her bedroom has a specific meaning. Faith is a deep, mysterious purple; the future a bright tangerine; friends are a stimulating twist of lime; family as important and blue as the night sky; love is the color of a valentine; and Beka herself identifies with the intensity of an Asian fuchsia blossom. As part of a large group of friends, Beka describes them as silver, like a precious metal:

We support each other with uplifting advice and encouragement.

The celebration of these personal values is the inspiration for Beka's room, not the latest magazine trend, or the personal preferences of her mother, who also happens to be a designer. Cherie, Beka's mom, and her dad, David, did however get splashed by their daughter's buoyant colors and values:

At first, when she told me what she wanted to do, I thought "Oooh myyyy gooosh, all that color!" It sounded fun and uplifting, but I got such negative feedback from everyone I told about it. They would be shocked and then say something like, "You used all of those colors at one time?!!!" And then there was Beka's desire to use a lot of black. My personal connotation of black is about death or that it is gothic. But she sees black as bringing contrast, harmony, and balance to the colorful setting. So, I had to challenge my own preconceptions because her reasoning was sound.

The adult peer pressure that Cherie experienced when she shared Beka's room scheme with friends is not unusual. These kinds of passive-aggressive comments (remarks weighted with personal agendas, experiences, and fears) by others can undermine our adult individuality as powerfully as the criticism of a haircut by a pack of eighth graders can sting a 13-year-old. Adult peer pressure and our need for acceptance are exactly what keep many of us from personal fulfillment. If we are ever going to become real again, like we were at seven or so, we must enter the same state of playful oblivion that allowed us to be creative at that age. Working with our children to nurture and maintain their creativity is one of the best means of rediscovering our own.

Stick to your guns and have faith in your (and your child's) ideas and vision. When you encounter more peer resistance, affirm to yourself, *"This is for a child's room, I can do whatever I want. After all, I don't want my child to ever lose his/her own creative freedom."* Or, if summoning "color courage" for your own room, try this affirmation: *"The spirit of the Creator is within me, therefore I am filled with Divine ideas!"* Also, we must believe that the Creator—the one that made colorful flowers and exotic birds—is within us. So, why wouldn't we, too, crave to paint in the color palette of an Amazon parrot? Jodi, Jessica's mom, shares how she developed color courage:

Just by focusing inward—toward your heart—you allow the beauty of God to take over, and your fears will go away. Instead of fixating on the negative comments you have received, reflect on what the colors and ideas mean to you or your child. Once you have a couple of projects accomplished, you will have much greater strength and belief in your own creative instincts.

When we face the disbelief of family and friends, especially when we are unearthing our *real-self*, it is comforting to be surrounded by other true believers. Cherie found a compatriot in her husband David. She is fortunate. Sometimes, the moms that I have worked with find that their husbands are resistant to colorful paint treatments, even nail holes. David, a master carpenter by profession who specializes in historic preservation, shares his advice with other fathers:

We don't want to discourage our kids' creativity. But we also should have respect for the architectural character of the house itself. In Beka's room, I built the bookshelves and moldings to be in keeping with the house's structure. The other elements that Beka designed—the bright tissue paper walls and lime green ceiling—could all be changed at a later time. That is a good criterion. If it can be changed without having to knock down walls, then it is acceptable. The paint, nail holes, furniture, slipcovers, and the rest can evolve and change as Beka does.

When I started to work with the Browns, I asked Beka to select colors to represent her core beliefs and values. She would then use those colors throughout her sacred place to tell her "heart story." The colorful heart-style the family of three created is told with stenciled pillows, confetti tissue paper walls, an affirmation slipcover, a friendship-celebrating stained-glass window, and more. These creative projects can be easily personalized for your own use. I have used many of these projects in my own home—to stay real with myself. There is nothing more joyful to the heart than being surrounded by one's own *True Colors*.

book of belief page: true colors

Begin by making a list of you and your child's favorite colors. Go to a paint or home store and pick out sample paint chips. Now, refer back to your list of values for life. Match a value with the color that best represents it. Add the chips to your Book of Belief. Start to imagine ways to incorporate them into your place. Beka made pillows and created amazing Technicolor walls to surround herself in the values by which she lives. Here's how you can too.

HAVE A CHAIR SIGNING PARTY: An autographed slipcover keeps good experiences and warm thoughts from close friends for years to come. Beka and her friends Carrie and Katy have a blast as they personalize a slipcover made by Beka's mom Cherie.

the proof is in the paint

Getting the exact color, technique, or feeling you want may require a few tries. I always use what I call the "Elizabeth Taylor Rule": give yourself up to nine times to get it right. Yes, really! Even after 20 years of practice, it usually takes me at least a couple of tries to get it right. One way to cut to the chase is by creating sample boards. These give you a chance to try patches of paint color or other treatments like Beka's tissue paper wall. You can use 2' x 2' pieces of Masonite or even heavy poster board for your trial run. Also, remember that color changes in different light. Be sure and try your choices in light comparable to the room you are planning.

"true colors" wall confetti and pillows

Rebeka started by identifying all of the colors that she loved. Each color was then given a meaning: purple for faith, red for love, lime green for friends, tangerine for the future, and so on. To keep these values in sight, she decided to surround herself with them, by making joyful confetti-strewn walls. Basic tissue paper was cut into 5" squares and applied to the wall surface with premixed wallpaper glue. She and her mom, Cherie, also added another dimension by making pillows in her true colors. Each pillow was stenciled with the value it represents. To do these projects with your child, start by completing the Book of Belief pages suggested above.

TRUE COLORS WALL CONFETTI: Beka cut 5" squares of tissue paper and applied them to her walls with strippable wallpaper paste.

HEART AND HANDS PROJECT

heart objective: To build and support identity and character by materially expressing them with color, paper, and fabric.

hands activity: For walls: Cut and apply tissue paper in an all-over pattern to one or more walls. For pillows: Buy or make pillows in your truest colors. Use stencil lettering and acrylic paint to label each pillow with its meaning.

steps to take: Detailed instructions found under True Colors Wall and Pillow photos.

"stained-glass" friends

There is nothing more sacred than a stained-glass window. For Rebeka, friendship is sacred and worthy of such a tribute. To enshrine her friends in color and light, we created our own version from colored Plexiglas squares. Images of her friends were copied onto transparency paper and then applied to the colored squares. The result is a light-catching window treatment that covers not only the window but also illuminates the soul.

STAINED-GLASS FRIENDS: Make photocopies of friends and others you love on transparency paper. Cut them out. Using a spray adhesive, fix them to Plexiglas squares. Use key chain to link the squares together.

HEART AND HANDS PROJECT

heart objective: Provides feelings of love, family, warmth, and belonging.

hands activity: Create a stained-glass type window covering using Plexiglas and transparency images.

steps to take: Detailed instructions found under Stained-Glass Friends photos.

POSITIVE REINFORCEMENT: An autographed chair, covered with positive messages from Beka's friends, provides a physically and spiritually comforting place of rest.

CHAPTER 6

the velveteen baby

What I didn't share with you previously is that Cherie and David Brown waited three years for their daughter Rebeka to arrive. When she finally came to them it was aboard the giant "Silver Stork", as her Grandpa Pearson called it, the jet that brought the baby all the way from her birthplace in Korea. Her father's memory of the little infant as she emerged from the plane is ignited when he recalls Garrison Keillor's narrative about the "Korean-Swede" baby (Cherie's family is of Swedish descent). Now that Beka is a bouyant 15-year-old enmeshed in school activities and learning to drive a car, her Korean heritage is currently of little more than casual interest. When asked about her parents, she explains:

Sometimes when people see me with my mom and dad—because we obviously look different—they ask thoughtless questions like "Have you ever met your real mom and dad?" To me these are my real parents. Real parents are the ones who give you love, patience, a sense of humor, courage, and direction.

WELCOME HOME: In the adopted baby Anna's nursery, handmade expressions of love and acceptance surround her.

Beka's dad, David, elaborates further:

One way a parent expresses love to his child is by teaching a belief-system. When you look at what makes us like one another or different, it is really more about our shared beliefs, values, and experiences than about a physical likeness. A belief-system gives a child an operating procedure by which they can successfully navigate through life. It should, of course, do so with love and tolerance.

Beka and David have added one more insight as to what truly makes us real. As parents, it is not necessarily our biology that matters, but the love that we *give.* In our earlier discussion of *The Velveteen Rabbit,* we acknowledged that the love we receive from our children can give us the courage to be ourselves. And as parents, it is the love that we give back that makes a baby *really* our own. The following story illustrates this truth.

a mother's longing

Four years earlier, Anna had started calling for her new parents, and Carla had heard her. Carla and Tom had always wanted a big family. Their two young boys had brought them so much happiness that they wanted more children, trying the old-fashioned way for a few years. Now in her late thirties, Carla attempted the in vitro fertilization process:

I went through it three different times. At the end I was devastated. I felt ripped apart and had this huge confrontation with God. I said to Him, "I don't want a million dollars or a big house. I just want to be a mother. Why do I have this maternal longing if I can't do this?"

Carla speaks for the feelings of so many women in their thirties and forties, especially now that we have been told that after age thirty it becomes much more difficult to become pregnant. Carla described her need as biological. She really wanted a biological child. So, she and Tom waited a year more. Then, she says, destiny unfolded:

I was at a PTA meeting and this lady with a beautiful baby sat down beside me. We started talking and I found out she was a foster parent. She looked into my eyes and said there are a lot of kids who need families, as many as 1,500 in any medium-sized city. So,

Tom and I decided to go through foster parent training. We got a call that there was a baby girl who needed a home. But there was a problem—she cried a lot.

The caseworkers said that the foster baby, Anna, did cry a lot—sometimes all night and all day. When Carla and Tom had gone to see her for the first time, the three-month-old was indeed crying. Yet, they decided to take her to their home for a visit anyway. They left equipped with a little bag of her essentials. The pair was prepared for a noisy night, Anna's reputation preceding her. Carla recounted:

We were so excited to have her in our home—and scared, too. We had made a snug little bed for her. When we put her in it she just nestled into the blankets. You could almost see a little smile of relief on her face—she felt at home. And guess what? She slept the whole night through! When we woke up and realized she hadn't cried, we ran in to see if she was okay. She just looked up and cooed. We knew then that, at least in heart, she was ours.

We all know that babies cry for a reason. They are hungry, don't feel well, or want to be held. It seems Anna was crying for her *real* parents, Carla and Tom. When she found them she stopped crying, except when she was taken away from them for visits with her birth parents. She would cry so hard then that she would make herself sick. These were also painful times for Carla and Tom. They would have to wait a period of a year to fully complete the adoption procedures. During that time, the birth parents could petition for custody.

home sweet home

For a long time, Carla could not bring herself to put Anna's things away. Her little knit shirts, all-in-ones, and socks stayed in the suitcase. Carla could not bear the thought of having to take them out, which—until the year-long wait had ended—was a very real possibility. One day when she was gone, however, she came home to find that Tom had done it for her. Anna was official. She had a chest of drawers of her own! And Carla's friend Bobbie was even encouraging her to begin to decorate the baby's room. She found art objects she thought Carla might like, including a guardian angel mobile that was irresistible. Carla soon was convinced to make a commitment to Anna's room, especially when her dear Aunt Jeanette became involved.

Jeanette, a wonderful decorative painter who had participated in my House of Belief workshop training, invited me into Anna's project. Like most mothers of infants, Carla's time was very limited. So, Jeanette volunteered to do much of the creative work, while I devised heart and hands projects that would help express the new family's feelings about their daughter and sister. As the day approached that Anna would legally become their daughter, everyone's feelings ran deep. I suggested that Carla and Tom each write a letter telling the little girl how they felt to have her in their family. The boys, Billy, 7, and Tommy, 11, also wrote notes to Anna. The parents' letters would then be heat-transferred onto a blanket-comforter. That way, Anna would literally become wrapped in their love. And later in life she would have a precious keepsake from her mom and dad. The boys' thoughts and pictures were transferred onto pillows, as well.

Here is what Carla wrote to Anna:

Dear Baby Girl:

As I lift you out of your bed each day, I am always amazed and overjoyed by your big toothy smile and dimples. You are the light of my life in so many ways. The first time I held you in my arms I knew I was supposed to be your mother. It was like I had been looking all over for you, then there you were. I had been waiting for you for so long and didn't even know it. I am certain you were meant to be my daughter.

I love you,

Momma

BABY, ME, AND TEA: The author created this ottoman/side table as a gift for Anna's mom. The skirt is made from a child's petticoat.

The baby's new father, Tom, wrote a letter of his own:

Dear Anna:

God has blessed me with two awesome boys. Now, He has put you in my life. You will be loved and protected, and grow up to have the best life I can offer you. I am looking forward to the day I will walk you down the aisle at your wedding.

Love,
Daddy

growing together

A**s we ventured further** into the decoration of Anna's bedroom, Carla got a chance to expand her own creative horizons. Aunt Jeanette once again became her mentor:

Jeanette has always been supportive of me even though I have never thought of myself as creative. Everyone in my family runs over with talents like cooking, needlework, baking, and art. I have always been very intimidated by it. I didn't even want to try creative things. When she suggested this wild lime green color for Anna's wall, I was worried it wouldn't fit with the rest of my earth-toned house. But she said that if I didn't like it we could paint over it. That is so true. It's just paint! Might as well give it a try; that is what I can easily say now as a result. And I love that green.

Carla says she is now more open to trying different things. She especially loves the raspberry slipcover that Jeanette made; it is comfortable for late night rocking. Also, she finds herself delighted by the petticoat table, perfect for books or a cup of tea for a weary mom. Baby Anna seems to be most excited by the nightlight lampshade that I made for her. She points to it and says, "Anna!" And she's right. I had her beautiful little face and hazel eyes in mind when I painted it. You can create any one of these heirloom projects for your-self, other parents, or a baby that you love. Simply fill in your own heartfelt symbols and meanings. Carla says, *"Oh, just give it a try!"*

If you are a new parent, this is a great time to meditate on all of those things you want your new baby to know now, and in the future. Think about your teaching points—those beliefs and values you would like to instill. These can be included in the room as reminders of your intentions as a parent. Carla and Tom are now rethinking their boys' rooms. They wish they had written welcome letters to the boys at birth. They would also like Billy and Tommy to have more physical representations of their love for them, like the letter-blanket, pillows, wall hanging, and stool. Even if your kids are older, it is never too late to do these heart and hands projects. Use the following questionnaire to formulate your teaching points, messages to your child, and reminders.

ANNA'S NIGHT LIGHT: This recycled lampshade was embellished with paint, glitter, and paper cutouts.

BABY, HERE IS WHAT YOU
SHOULD KNOW . . .

✻ How it feels for us as parents, to have you in our lives:

✻ Here are three beliefs about your young life to guide
you:

✻ Above all else, value these things:

✻ When life gets hard, here is how we will help you:

✻ If you can remember just one thing, it is this:

✻ When it comes to fulfilling your dreams, here is how
we will help:

BELIEF STATEMENT: A recycled window frame outlines a punched metal statement of belief.

a "love letter" blanket

When a child comes into our lives, we can be overwhelmed with so many feelings. A new birth—the very spirit of creativity itself in a little human form—can arouse our own needs to express all of the love, joy, and hope that we are experiencing. Committing these feelings to paper, and then to a blanket, quilt, or comforter, will keep them real and alive for both you and your child.

HEART AND HANDS PROJECT

heart objective: To express our love, joy, and gratitude—now and forever.

hands activity: Write a letter or note and then heat-transfer it to fabric for a blanket or comforter.

steps to take: Detailed instructions found under Love Letter Blanket photo.

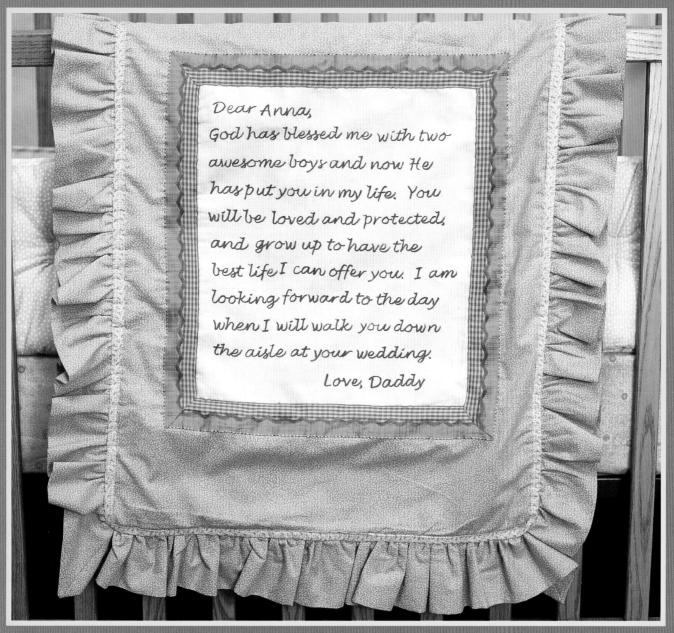

Dear Anna,
God has blessed me with two awesome boys and now He has put you in my life. You will be loved and protected, and grow up to have the best life I can offer you. I am looking forward to the day when I will walk you down the aisle at your wedding.

Love, Daddy

A LOVE LETTER BLANKET: Parents Carla and Tom each wrote letters to their new adopted baby, telling her how they feel now that she is in their lives. The letters were then heat-transferred onto a blanket.

do a "diaper" wall glaze

Kids are rumored to do very creative things with their diapers, and sometimes with what is in them! Don't worry; this wall treatment uses paint, not other substances. This glazing effect is so fun and easy, even busy new moms will have time to try it. Anna's Aunt Jeanette has taken a complicated procedure and reduced it to three simple steps. It is so easy that the baby could do-it-herself!

DO A DIAPER GLAZE: On a white wall, paint on the acrylic color you prefer. Your paint should be the consistency of syrup—thinner than it is when you open the can. While it is wet, use a soft clean diaper, held bunched-up, to dab the wall, making a soft mottled pattern.

HEART AND HANDS PROJECT

heart objective: To empower a parent's own creativity and provide feelings of commitment to our child's creative development.

hands activity: Select a color and transform at least one wall with the diaper glaze treatment.

steps to take: Detailed instructions found next to Diaper Wall Glaze photos.

On the pillow photo:

Anna Banana is Special

I Love my Sister

Anna is a cute sister

I Love Anna

Billy M.

PILLOW BUDDIES: Tommy and Billy made photo pillows with special messages to welcome their new sister.

CHAPTER

a mirror of her soul

Jasmine Tinner's bedroom is like a richly imagined poem, or maybe, an anthology of short stories. There are furniture phrases, mirror metaphors, and pillow protagonists. There is even a giant book cover or two with titles hinting at the young writer's favorite themes. Underfoot, painted right on the old wood floor is a book jacket that we created together for her story called, *Just Like Me.* On the cover is a big oval, gold-gilt mirror with Jasmine's reflection in it. In the foreground there is another girl, or woman, looking into the mirror. She has red hair that is woven into braids, and she looks, well, just like me. Materializing in the background of the mirror are the words, "We are all reflections of each other." Jasmine explains her story:

> There is a girl named Jasmine, and she has a pen pal she writes to, named Samantha. They get to know each other through their letters. Jasmine believes her friend is just like her—in color and age—because they like all of the same things. Finally, one day they get to meet. Samantha is an older white lady! So, Jasmine starts to believe that skin color and age don't really matter, because inside we all look the same.

INNER REFLECTION: Jasmine created a mirror that provides a place of personal inner reflection. The inscription reads: "A mirror of the soul . . . what do you see?"

Here is a mystical example of life imitating art, or vice versa. Essentially, it is the story of Jasmine and me. Through our friendship, we have found that we have so much in common, despite the difference in culture and age. Our creativity is our common bond. And what is true for us is true for all people. Though we may have different life experiences, we all have the same spirit of the Creator within us. When we come to realize that our "differences" are just that creative spirit—the Master Artist—expressing uniquely through us, we have a common ground for respect and understanding. This belief inspired me to create a heart and hands project many years ago called *A Soul Mirror*. I invited Jasmine to try it for herself as a further expression of her own beliefs.

There are two ways to create a soul mirror, and we did them both. First, we made a wall mirror into a place of personal reflection. Posing the question to viewers: "This is a mirror of the soul, what do you see?" The challenge is to look into the reflection of your own eyes and honestly acknowledge what you see: the good and the not-so-good. The second step is to make a soul mirror pendant: a symbol that when worn, serves to remind us that we are all reflections of each other. When others approach the wearer, they can sometimes see themselves reflected back at them. You can find more details about how you and your child can create your own soul mirrors later in the chapter.

writing her own story

Jasmine, who is now 12, has been committing her thoughts to paper for as long as she has known how to write. Already, she has compiled a thick notebook of poems and short stories. Born with a sage's wisdom and a prophet's need to share and enlighten, her themes have never been compatible with her young age. At eight-years-old she wrote a short story, called *The Life of Tina Frances June*, about a young girl's experiences with racism. I met her that year and could never have guessed that behind her warm-as-May sunshine smile, such deep thoughts were stirring. They say that like attracts like: she and I became fast friends.

Using tissue paper, wood medallions, and mirrors, Jasmine and her great-grandmother Gloria brought a worn-out dresser back to life.

Shortly thereafter, Jasmine's mom, Sheandrika, took a job in another state. I was saddened by the distance, but I kept track of her progress through her great-grandmother, my good friend, Gloria. I had come to know the whole family through their participation in the House of Belief workshops I hosted in our community. But soon our relationship eclipsed the Saturday afternoon creative sessions they attended. Before I knew it, we were all having Gloria's world-class barbeque on their front porch. I was honored to be included in this family of five living generations of women, privy to more than 100 years of valuable experiences.

When Jasmine returned to our city a few years later, I saw a marked difference in her demeanor. Before, her face was an open horizon, and you felt you could walk its distance. Now, at age 11, the open plain had been divided up by walls; barriers erected for personal safety. In this verse from her poem, *"Hide,"* she explained the changes:

> *I hide my answers from you because yours might be better.*
>
> *I hide my truth from you because you say it's a lie.*

Jasmine says that when you are small, people are supportive of your ideas. They give you encouragement. But as you get older, they are much more critical. It becomes harder to be yourself, because you are afraid of being laughed at or ridiculed. She says this has happened to her both at school and in her family, although she knows that her family has never meant to intentionally hurt her. It is true; we can become very casual, cynical, and even suspicious about imaginative notions. I first experienced this when I was seven.

truth or fiction?

In my first grade class, we were reading the story of Cinderella. I went home and told my mom that I was Cinderella in the play at school. I *did* read the part in my class. My mom jumped to the conclusion that there was to be a full-scale production and I was its star. I easily fell into the story—and why not? I was going to be a star! Before you knew it, my parents had me calling the whole family to invite them to the play. As the day approached, I became fearful. I didn't want to let them down. Of course, when they found out that there was no play, was I ever in trouble! My imagination was said to be "out-of-control," and became the suspect in every household crime. At least, that is how I perceived it.

Clearly, kids need to be able to distinguish between fantasy and reality. I hear parents say, *"My child's imagination is really scary . . . the things he can think up."* Some parents worry that a child's wild and imaginative stories portend of some wicked tendency to lie. So, they padlock the young mind for good. Be cautious: our words and actions can help that imagination to paint a better world or enslave it to the cold hard facts. We can do the latter, unintentionally discouraging our kids' mind's eye ramblings without ever realizing it. However, there are positive statements that will help you to inspire a healthy and responsible imagination in your children. Here are some suggestions:

- ❋ When responding to a story, say: "That's a great story. How does it differ from real life?" or "Those ideas are very creative, where did they come from?" My answer, for example, about the Cinderella story might have been, "Well, Mom, you gave me a lot of help . . ." (Smile, wink.)

- ❋ Give your child a compliment and provide them with a distinction between fun and truthfulness: "Honey! You have the mind of a great writer or artist; you will go far in life. When artists are working, they think creatively, just like you."

- ❋ To help a child take responsibility for their story, without accusing them of lying, say, "Did your answer come from your high mind, where the Creator's ideas live, or from somewhere else?" You may also give them logical help out of their error. If they say they finished their homework at school (and you know they didn't) say, "Let's look it over together, it will be more fun that way."

THE LIFE OF TINA
FRANCES JUNE

In 1939 Marian Anderson performed at the Lincoln Memorial. Marian also published her first book titled My Lord, What A Morning in 1956. She spent many years singing and studying music in Europe. Also, she was invited to sing at the White House for Presidents Kennedy and Eisenhower.

HARRIET TUBMAN
ANTISLAVERY ACTIVIST
M. W. Taylor

When a child is sharing dreams or ideas for the future, always respond positively. You can ask, *"What will you do to make those things happen for yourself?"* This will suggest that dream fulfillment is a personal responsibility.

A bumper sticker I've seen reads: *Those who have given up on their own dreams are very happy to help you give up on yours.* We simply must not put our own limitations on our child's imagination, no matter how far out of our own personal realm of accomplishment or experience they are. I believe we all do the best in rearing our children that we know how to do at the time. So, be kind to yourself. And if you feel your own parents may have not done right by you, follow these four steps: look, learn, forgive, and then move on quickly.

tv or not tv?

When we read a book, we lucidly imagine or see with our mind's eye the characters' faces, their clothing, and the setting. No filmed version can compare to J.K. Rowling's description of the despicable Dursleys—Harry Potter's foster family. As I watched the movie, I kept looking for the breakfast eggs that always stick in the father's mustache and a mother so horse-faced (as the author describes her) you expect her to whinny. That is how I saw them when I read the book. The movie might as well have been acted out by puppets and shot in black and white compared to what I had envisioned.

One of the most dangerous influences on a young imagination is watching too much television. Television can turn off the original creative mind within your child—and in the worst cases, make them morally confused.

Researchers say that the human mind, especially in the young, has a hard time distinguishing between what it has seen happening on television and what it has really experienced. The imprinting on our minds of what we see in video form is so extensive that we can accept it as fact, especially when we are little. For example, if a child sees someone killed or brutalized in cartoons, movies, or video games, and then sees the character get up and walk away, that child may come to believe that there are no consequences to death. Someone can be battered or killed and still seem to remain alive.

BELIEVE AND ACHIEVE: At her writing desk, Jasmine is reminded of other women who have believed and achieved: her chair features the opera singer Marian Anderson. The photo and text were applied using the heat-transfer technique.

I have always wondered what the long-term effects of this kind of television watching has on kids. The information I found is startling. John Murray, Director of the School of Family Studies, at Kansas State University, explains:

The long-term effects of programming with violent content may be for kids to be less sensitive to pain and suffering in others, more fearful of the world around them, and have more aggressive behavior toward others.

WOMEN-TO-BELIEVE-IN PILLOWS: Thanks to a Styrofoam headboard and valance kit from Create-It-Décor, Jasmine and Gloria were able to make a matching set for the girl's room. Inspiring women are featured on the pillows they also made, including: Bessie Coleman, Debbie Allen, and Maya Angelou.

HEAT TRANSFER PILLOWS: Images of inspiring women were first photocopied on heat-transfer paper, then ironed onto the cotton fabric. Finally, Jasmine and Gloria sewed the fabric into pillows.

Time Magazine family columnist Amy Dickinson reports that two-thirds of all kids eight and older have a television in their bedrooms. And a third of kids, ages two to seven, have TVs in their rooms. The data from this study, she says, shows that television viewing is becoming an increasingly private and isolating activity. So, essentially what we have are kids alone in their bedrooms, turning off their imaginations to the creativity of *make and believe*-style play and flipping the on-switch to violence and other questionable imagery.

Statistics show that there are about five acts of violence committed in one hour of prime time programming and 20 to 25 acts that occur each hour on Saturday morning "children's programs." And kids, who watch four or more hours a day, put in less effort at school, have poorer reading skills, participate in fewer hobbies and interests, and do not play as well with others.

Based on this information, *I strongly recommend excluding the television set, computer, and Gameboy from your child's bedroom.* This will give your kids the space to formulate their own thoughts and invent their own safe and serene worlds. Throughout this book, we have seen kids making their rooms into sacred places of creativity and belief. As their imaginations unfurl, they write their own original stories on the "pages" of their bedroom. Codes of conduct, lists of intentions, and creeds of character take shape on walls, windows, and furniture. Each of these kids has written their own belief story and handmade it into a three-dimensional book called *Me.*

jasmine's book of me

By looking at Jasmine's bedroom, you can see into her soul, and a little of her great-grandma Gloria's, too. On many of the *heart and hands projects* they worked side-by-side, Glo's sewing skills helping to bring form to the curtains, pillows, and headboard. In creating the tissue paper and mirror-covered dresser, the two also worked together. Gloria, a retired substance abuse counselor, sees great merit in the process:

> *It is self-esteem building. It allows you to look into yourself and find abilities that you didn't know you   had. Jasmine has grown herself up by being creative. She has become self-motivated. She thinks about something and takes her hands and produces what she is thinking about. Though she has always been independent, it has helped her self-confidence.*

A GIFT TO ME BOXES: Jasmine created gift boxes to symbolically represent what she intends to give herself in life.

Jasmine likes to people her book with women she admires, including Bessie Coleman, Maya Angelou, Debbie Allen, and Marian Anderson. Pictures of these role models have been heat-transferred to pillows. She says it is encouraging to share her space with such brave faces:

My favorite is Marian Anderson. She wasn't afraid of anything. She made her own concert at the Lincoln Memorial when she was turned down at a concert hall because of her skin color. She never gave up on her dreams and always kept striving. No one kept her from being herself.

But of all the things she has created, her *"A Gift to Me"* boxes are her favorite, she says:

I got to be the true me when I made my boxes. Sometimes I messed them up, but I kept trying. They would always turn out better than I first imagined. The final touches made the transformation complete. Really, with the whole room it was like when I write a story. At first I don't have the whole picture. One idea brings more. It just takes patience.

And then before you know it, you have a whole story—or room—accomplished.

write a "belief story": paint a book cover!

Jasmine has now added further stock to her vessel of self: a giant-sized book, all written and painted (with assistance from me) on the floor of her bedroom. Her hands went to work to illustrate the good ideas of her heart in a visible form. The constancy of it always in sight in her bedroom will serve as a reminder of the belief she holds and her goal of becoming a writer. Jasmine says, " I just can't stop looking at that book cover. I like it so much. I feel good about what I did whenever I see it."

GIFT GIVING: Jasmine's gift boxes are symbolic *and* practical. Every teenager needs a place for special things.

HEART AND HANDS PROJECT

heart objective: To express a positive belief or experience for your child's life by creating and /or illustrating a story about it.

hands activity: Write down a belief you or your child has and why you have it. Now, ask where your child's belief came from. Think of stories you know which help to represent the belief. Think of the lesson or message you want your child or others to know from reading the story. Draw and then paint the book cover that represents your child's belief-story.

steps to take: With your child, write, paint, or draw the story on your walls, canvas, paper, or floor. Plan how it will lay out on the wall or canvas. Do sketches and take measurements to make sure it will work. And remember, this is not the Sistine Chapel; it is a child's room. Success lies in allowing your child to express him/herself, and it is the process of self-discovery that is most important, not a gallery product. If you do feel you need help with the artistry, find a painter or artist who can help get you started. Art schools are great for finding students that might assist you and your child.

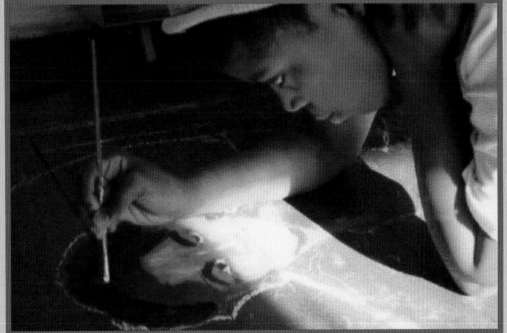

WRITE A BELIEF STORY, PAINT A BOOK COVER: Start from a sketch you have drawn. Enlarge it to the size it will appear on the floor or other surface. Using carbon tracing paper, transfer the drawing to the floor. Acrylic paints are recommended to color in the drawing. To preserve your work, coat 1–3 times with polyurethane sealer.

A FOUNDATION OF BELIEF: On the floor of her bedroom, Jasmine and the author painted giant boo
stories that Jasmine is writing.

make a "soul mirror" pendant

Even though we may look different from our neighbors on the outside, inside we look the same. "We are reflections of each other" is the simple message contained in Jasmine's pendant. A smaller version of the Soul Mirror that she made for her bedroom, the pendant is guaranteed to create feelings of harmony with both friends and strangers.

HEART AND HANDS PROJECT

heart objective: To serve as a visual reminder of our love and respect for others.

hands activity: Using the Soul Mirror kit, decorate your mirror to represent your own unique creative spirit.

SOUL MIRROR PENDANTS: Jasmine and the author wear their symbols of creative unity. The pendant reminds us that we are all, even though we look different, reflections of each other.

CHAPTER 8

alex's rite of passage

Alex Berkovich, age 10, was sure he had met Draco Malfoy, the cruel, young wizard who had menaced his hero, Harry Potter. Everyday for weeks, he had been harassed by this schoolyard "dark magician" who had cast a spell over Alex so potent that the Harry look-alike became sick. Every Monday morning his stomach turned with dread:

I just didn't want to go to school. I couldn't take being made fun of any longer. That kid picked on me all the time because I had allergies. I felt so bad about myself, I just didn't want to go on. I didn't know what to do.

Some experts say that this kind of bullying is part of what makes kids learn to navigate through the world, to develop survival skills early. I strongly disagree. I don't believe it is ever right for kids to have to face unkindness. Ideally, every family would teach the "good magic" of understanding, empathy, and compassion. If it were so, these kinds of schoolyard scenes would become obsolete behavior.

GOAL-ORIENTED: Alex's love of soccer is represented by a soccer goal headboard, which also keeps him focused on his game. Trophies are kept close by to remind him of his successes.

Sure, all of us face challenges: at school, in our work, or within our personal life that will ultimately make us stronger. If nothing else, these experiences provide distinctions by which we make choices as to what is right and wrong, how people should be treated, and what we enjoy doing with our lives. For example, an unappreciative boss can make us determined to be our own boss and nudge us toward our dream of self-employment. Illness can drive us to a new appreciation of the joy of having good health. In Alex's case, however, he already knew in his heart that words had the power of magic in them, causing a paralyzing, fearful illusion to fall over their recipient or wounding a tender young heart. Conversely, he also knew that when used by a good wizard, words can make us believe in ourselves and lift us from being just ordinary to heroic. Words accompanied by positive actions are the most powerful of all. Alex remembered:

The best day of my life, so far, was when I was eight. I was the first one on my team to catch a ball. My dad was really proud of me. Everyone congratulated me, too.

Words of encouragement can be a powerful antidote to even the darkest spell, especially when accompanied by visual proof that the negative thought or experience is wrong or can be overcome. We must, therefore, be surrounded with evidence of the truth about our children or ourselves. Alex keeps his sports trophies in sight, as well as posters of his favorite athletes. Visual reminders of our beliefs, values, goals, and dreams will keep us from falling into the negative illusions that can come from the outside world. One of the most empowering rituals of belief involves identifying our heroes and role models, those who may have shared some of our experiences, the good or bad, and went on to greatness. Images of these inspiring people keeps us living in the belief that what they accomplished for themselves, we can, too.

choose your ancestors

Harry Potter and all of the kids at the Hogwart's School have their own version of trading cards: paparazzi shots of the most powerful and glamorous wizards. (Our kids barter for star athletes or Pokemon favorites.) And the multilevel, open staircase at

A MEN-TO-BELIEVE-IN LAMP: This lamp reminds Alex of other men from history who were tested, yet triumphant. Alex and his dad are included, affirming their own greatness.

Harry's school is hung heavily with ancestral portraits (not necessarily true relatives of the students) that can come to life and impart advice or wisdom. In my house, I have my own version of this gallery. Do you have a gallery of role models for you and your child?

I have a saying, "Choose your ancestors": those people to whom you feel a spiritual connection. My sacred place has been shared by Beethoven, Marian Anderson, William Blake, Rosa Parks, William Morris, Jane Austen, and others. They have been included in paintings or on picture postcards, tucked here and there, and have lived in biographies I've read about them. *Remember that when it is in sight, it is in mind.* The vision of Rosa Parks makes me bold in my resolve to do what I personally believe in. The sound of Beethoven's "Seventh Symphony" reminds me that the Creator always finds a way to bring beauty into our lives, no matter what is happening (the composer was becoming deaf when he wrote this piece). Of course, the pictures don't literally talk to me, *but they do communicate much.*

These spiritual ancestors bring us the power of belief. Kids especially need to make their own family of role models, those who can help give them the courage to go to school, and survive it. Many ancient cultures, from China to the Native American traditions, celebrate "rites of passage" for young men and women when they are close to or going through adolescence. These acts are meant to empower a child with courage and wisdom, transitioning them to capable adults. The young initiates are believed to be guided by the spirits of their deceased ancestors and the living elders in the group. You see, they have role models—those upon which to pattern themselves. Today, we live without many traditions or rituals that help **kids to envision** themselves as brave, powerful, and strong.

men who believed

I started Alex on his first heart and hands project by asking him about his favorite heroes. Not surprisingly, his dad topped the list:

To describe my dad, you could use any word that means good or perfect. He is always there for me; he coaches me at soccer and other sports. I don't think I could make it without his support. He is everything that a hero should be.

MEN-TO-BELIEVE-IN WINDOW SHADE: Like Jasmine's pillows, this shade peoples Alex's view with inspiring role models. They include Gandhi, John F. Kennedy, Martin Luther King, Jr., Chief Black Elk, Satchel Paige, and others.

Then, I invited Alex and his dad to work with me to find some new role models besides the "athletes of the moment" he had named. We began by making a list of Alex's other interests and intentions. This evaluation helped us to seek out great men who were in those categories. Men he could relate to and be inspired by. Once he selected his icons, we would feature their pictures on a *Men-To-Believe-In Shade*. We also made a matching lamp. Here are his selections and why he chose them:

Alex's Interest: SCIENCE
Heroes: STEPHEN HAWKING, ALBERT EINSTEIN

Hawking, a pioneer in the theory of black holes, is arguably the most famous scientist since Einstein. Hawking has the distinction of being almost completely immobile and confined to a wheelchair as a result of ALS, a motor neuron disease. Einstein, the father of modern relativity, was once believed to have been learning impaired.

Alex's Belief: NONVIOLENCE, DIVERSITY
Heroes: MAHATMA GANDHI, DR. MARTIN LUTHER KING, JR.

Gandhi, best known for his nonviolent efforts to liberate the people of India, met with much personal abuse in his lifetime. His experiences with bigotry motivated him to be a leader for fairness. And Dr. King's social movement for racial equality in America was also effective through nonviolent protests.

Alex's Value: ENVIRONMENT, RECYCLING
Hero: CHIEF BLACK ELK

Known for his prophecies, this Lakota Sioux Chief has brought forth much sacred wisdom on our environment and what we must do to save it.

Alex's Dream: TO BE AN ATHLETE OR PHYSICAL EDUCATION TEACHER
Hero: SATCHEL PAIGE

Paige was the star of the Kansas City Monarchs in the Negro Baseball League. Despite much hardship, he made the best of his career and used sports as a platform for communicating his beliefs.

book of belief pages: heroes, role models

Following the lead of Alex and his dad, help your child pick out his/her favorite people—those who inspire. First, identify one of their interests, beliefs, values, goals, or dreams. Then find a role model that exemplifies each one. Include them in your book and be sure to state why you chose them.

sports, of course

As surely as Harry Potter loves a game of Quidditch, so do most of our boys and girls love any kind of ballgame. We are told it's a positive thing, too, that kids who play organized sports are less likely to get into trouble. And if we listen to or read about the personal strategies of many successful athletes, it is easy to find techniques that can be adapted for "home use" in raising winning kids. One such concept originated in the story of Tara Lipinski.

You may recall the young Olympic gold medal ice skater who grabbed her prize at the tender age of 15. When asked about her win, she reported that she had been visualizing it since she was very small. It seems her parents had helped her to make a winner's platform on which to stand. As she did so, she would see, in her mind's eye, the Olympic gold medal being placed around her neck. She had gone through this exercise of *make and then believe* for years until it really happened.

Tiger Woods has talked about a similar approach. One of his personal heroes was the golf legend Jack Nicklaus. When Tiger was younger, he would keep a copy of Nicklaus's golf scores on his bedroom wall. He would look at them daily, aspiring at first to match them and then to top them. This wasn't a casual activity. Tiger would put great emotion and desire into his visualization, seeing himself do better than his hero had done. He knew the creative magic of belief.

"The best day of my life, so far, was when I was eight. I was the first one on my team to catch a ball. My dad was really proud of me. Everyone congratulated me, too."

Inspired by examples like these, Alex's stepmom, Jodi, set out to help the young soccer player see himself as a winner. Doing away with his traditional headboard, she installed a soccer goal in its place. Alex, when he is tucked in at night, is a goal himself—and headfirst! Talk about feeling like a winner, and for eight hours a night, too.

Jodi and Alex worked together to further surround the boy in a personally empowering atmosphere that would serve as a safe and secure haven, protected from schoolyard threats. They stamped fabrics with soccer images and created a playing field carpet with AstroTurf and tape. To express Alex's strong patriotic feelings, they painted pillowcases with the stars and stripes. Every young wizard needs an animal to help him out. Harry Potter had an owl. Alex Berkovich chose the eagle. He explains why:

> *The eagle is powerful, with a sharp eye. It represents strength and safety to me. I want to be like the eagle.*

"men-to-believe-in" window shade and lamp

Alex had been having trouble with mean kids at school. As a chess-playing sensitive boy, he was the frequent target of bullies. As a result, his self-esteem was crumbling. To help him keep his role models in mind, we created a window shade collage of inspiring men who had been bullied, and yet succeeded. The images he selected were: Gandhi, Einstein, Galileo, Chief Black Elk, Satchel Paige, John F. Kennedy, Martin Luther King, Stephen Hawking, and his own dad. Better not forget the one most important picture on the shade—Alex himself.

To bring an end to the worry many kids feel over future encounters with bullies we must address the root cause. Our kids need to feel safe at home and on the playground. For additional information on bullying; including tips and how-to resources for stopping the problem outside the home, please go to: www.houseofbelief.com

MEN-TO-BELIEVE-IN SHADE AND LAMP: To a vinyl or fabric window shade or lampshade, apply photocopied images of inspiring people. Use spray adhesive to fix them in place. Ribbon or other cording may be used to finish the edges.

HEART AND HANDS PROJECT

heart objective: To build self-belief and esteem by providing evidence that a child can succeed because others have done so.

hands activity: Apply photocopied images of inspiring people to a vinyl window shade and/or lampshade.

steps to take: Detailed instructions found under Men-To-Believe-In Window Shade and Lamp photos.

painting "fabrics of life"

Nothing can be more reassuring or life-giving than being surrounded by colors, patterns, and symbols that are meaningful to you. As it did in Alex's room, painting your own fabrics says, "I know who I am, I can make what I need, I am strong, resourceful, and courageous." Refer to your child's Book of Belief for colors and sacred symbols to paint on *Fabrics of Life*.

PAINT FABRICS OF LIFE: Using textile paint, stripe or stamp uplifting symbols to smooth cotton fabric. For stripes, apply masking tape and paint between taped lines. Pull back the tape to reveal the stripes. Be sure and try some samples first.

HEART AND HANDS PROJECT

heart objective: To give validity and support to personal identity and intentions by representing them in a material form.

hands activity: Stamp or stripe fabrics with favorite colors and symbols.

steps to take: Detailed instructions found under Fabrics of Life photos.

CHAPTER 9

butterfly dreams

Butterflies emerge from an environment that was inside of them all along. During their adolescence, which is the third of four life stages, the chrysalis or cocoon springs forth as the young caterpillar sheds away. Going deeper inside itself, the chrysalis tent billowing around it, the butterfly develops within the little silk room or cocoon. One day, when it is ready to "go and see the world," the adult will come out of its room, spread its wings, and fly away. This is the life cycle of butterflies and of our own children.

When I met Margaret Rowzee, she was ready to bring out an environment in which to surround herself. She quietly moved from one creative project to the next, as if she were irresistibly pulled through natural stages beyond her control, compelled by unseen but vocal "guiding forces." Imagination prompted, "I would like to travel to exotic places flitting about like a butterfly." Creativity answered, "Start now and make a cocoon from which you can spin your dreams." Then, Belief—remembering back to former accomplishments—added, "There is a lamp in your parent's attic. Get it and transform it into a sacred candle to burn bright for your dream." Imagination became really excited and said, "Yes! Yes! And what about all of that old jewelry you have been buying at thrift stores?"

A CONFIDENCE COCOON: Rather than buying expensive decorations for her room, Margaret's creativity has transformed her space. It is an outer reflection of her inner abilities.

Imagination—Creativity—Belief—Imagination—Creativity—Belief—Imagination— Creativity—Belief . . . This is the healthy cycle of development inside the human cocoon. The mind "envisions" an idea, creativity "makes" it real, and belief is increased by "seeing" the outcome. Within our homes is an environment providing young and old caterpillars alike with the necessary elements to become butterflies— an environment that promotes this spiritual cycle of transformation. As a child repeats this cycle, again and again through the process of "making" what he/she needs for their rooms, they are feeding their inner butterfly, and growing it to be independent, self-reliant, and free.

In Margaret's room, those necessary elements include beads, butterflies, and belief. Beads from thrift store jewelry are placed with intention on a lamp base. Each one signifies an action taken by Margaret of personal creativity and resourcefulness. The finished lamp reminds its 14-year-old maker that she is a child of the Creator and has the power to do for her whole life what she did with a cast-off lamp.

not an aladdin's lamp

So very different is that lamp of Margaret's from the Aladdin's lamp of Arabian legend. In that tale, a lamp is the home of a genie. Through releasing the genie, you can get what you ask for—in three wishes. Margaret's lamp tells a whole different story:

In life, I have the power to make what I want and need. My parents need not buy me expensive stuff. I don't expect anyone to do it for me. What I need, my creativity, comes from inside me. I can make what I wish to have in life.

Self-reliance and personal responsibility are what every parent wants for their child. These attributes are so highly valued that in many parent surveys, they rank first and second in qualities to be attained.

CREATIVE SELF-RELIANCE: Following the lead of her parents, Margaret uses her creativity rather than finances to make what she needs for life. A lamp found in the attic became a bejeweled expression of her resourcefulness.

That's ideal. But for some, the worst scenario they can envision is fighting for refrigerator or sofa space with a 30-year-old who "just can't find a job that's right for me"; and "by the way, my Reeboks are worn out, can I borrow your credit card?" In our time, gold charge cards contain the genie and the power of immediate gratification. Like Aladdin's lamp, wishes are granted at a very high price. For parents, the temptation of credit spending takes an even greater toll on our kids by teaching them a false lesson. The lesson that what we need in life, for personal fulfillment, for personal happiness, must come from our credit line or bank account.

In truth, our fulfillment and power comes from within. The spiritual currency of creativity and belief can, in fact, buy us the life of our dreams. If we want our children to grow up to be self-reliant and resourceful, we must also strive to live that way. Kids learn best by watching their parents. Because my own father constructed an addition to our small house, with his own hands, when I was a child, I further believed in my own abilities to make what I needed in life. I watched him struggle for months to complete a two-story project. The rain poured through the open roof, and we washed dishes in the bathtub for a while, but he achieved his goal. He drew a plan, gathered his materials, and sawed and hammered. In the end, we had a mansion! Or so it seemed to us. And I became empowered to someday make a home of my own.

Creating an atmosphere that nudges a young butterfly toward independence takes a commitment to live more creatively and less dependently ourselves. It is easy to see why Margaret is spreading her wings with such ease because her parents have shown her how.

MAKE-IT-YOURSELF AND THEN BELIEVE-IN-YOURSELF: Creative projects empowered Margaret's self-confidence. Here, she uses glass paint to add color and pattern to her bedroom windows.

BUTTERFLY AFFIRMATION PILLOW: This heart and hands project encourages us to affirm who we are becoming in life.

the butterfly school

The Rowzee household could easily be a butterfly training school, with degrees available in creativity and independence. Andy, Margaret's dad, and her stepmom, Laura, are creative self-starters. Operating a successful upholstery and slipcover business out of their home, the couple's days are filled with ideas, plans, actions, and accomplishments. Margaret has seen the necessity of follow-through—how to take a creative idea from start to finish. On any given day, she also witnesses miracles. Furniture that many people have given up on—wobbly, beaten-up, and worn-out—becomes miraculously transformed by the Rowzees' healing touch. The lesson: creativity and action can transform a chair, or any other aspect of your life. Andy puts it this way:

> *By watching our working process, Margaret has seen that an idea is only as good as the follow-through to bring it to fruition. She has realized that wishing and hoping are not the same as actually acting on your ideas.*

Besides a course in Follow-Through 101, the two parents also offer "classes" in thriftiness and resourcefulness for their daughter. Perusing flea markets and thrift stores together, the family relies on their imaginations, more often than their bank account. In their kitchen, for example, colorful plastic cups, purchased at a discount center, have become globes for light fixtures. And the floor is covered with a piece of canvas, painted in an abstract design by Andy. With creative expression valued above all else, they cull their materials from the most inexpensive places—sometimes even the curb. Retrieving other people's cast-offs, they make them uniquely their own with fabric, trimmings, and paint. I must admit that I, also, love to "curb shop" and have found some of my favorite things at sidewalk "stores." Besides exciting one's own imagination, it is also good for the environment. Be sure to add recycling to your young butterfly's course load.

Andy explains the outcome of such training:

Through projects at our house and at her mom's, which is her primary residence, I believe she has gained great confidence. Her mom, Susan, is also very creative. Margaret has traveled with her to artist Georgia O'Keefe's Ghost Ranch for inspiration. We would all say that Margaret has always been quietly creative. But now she is more forthcoming with her opinions. This is very positive for her—to be able to articulate how she feels about things.

Inside the Rowzee creative cocoon, materials from glue guns to paint are always within Margaret's reach. To promote spontaneous actions of creativity with your child, start by having tools and materials readily available. If you have to go to the store when you or your child has a creative idea, you may risk losing the inspiration of the moment. Who has time for all that running around anyway? We are always endeavoring to find ways to spend more sacred time at home with our families, in simple and meaningful ways. Let's make it as easy as possible. Here is one of my favorite solutions for having your materials always on hand: make a *Creativity Cabinet.*

a creativity cabinet

Like an art studio in a cabinet, this convenient place to store your family's creative materials will keep you responding to your ideas almost instantaneously. Start by thinking of where you will place it in your home. Of course, it could go in one of the kid's rooms. However, I would suggest a more prominent location, such as your family room or living room. Its very presence in such an important location states your intention to be more creative with the kids, perhaps as an alternative to watching too much television, or as a process of family sharing and communication. A living room, therefore, becomes more than a "watching" room. It really begins to live again through family fun.

A CREATIVITY CABINET: This whimsical container for art supplies keeps family creativity close at hand.

Why not make a *Creativity Cabinet* as a family gift for Christmas, or as a birthday idea for one of the kids? The creation of the cabinet and materials to put inside it will provide an immediate family experience together, and more for the future. I have listed below some essential items to store in it. You may already have many of them.

- 2 sets of watercolor markers—one permanent
- 1 scale ruler
- Rubber and foam stamps—assorted
- Acrylic paints—assorted colors
- Glue sticks, a glue bottle
- Ribbons, cord, and trim
- Tissue paper—mixed colors
- 1 package heat-transfer paper
- A few yards of raw canvas fabric
- Masking tape—various sizes
- Pie tins for paint palettes

- 1 set of 24 colored pencils
- 2 scissors
- Stamp pads
- Brushes—assorted sizes
- Glue gun—low temperature
- Assorted colorful craft papers
- A hole punch
- A few yards of off-white cotton fabric.
- Paper towels, wax paper
- Jars for water

The creativity cabinet I made recently was as fun and meaningful as any other heart and hands project. I started with a $60 yard sale buffet that I purchased from my neighbors, two doors down. In keeping with the thought that *kids are butterflies in the making and creative materials make their cocoons complete,* I used a butterfly motif for my central design. I asked my friend, Eric, to help me put together a simple three-shelf bookcase with a butterfly opening in the center. That part of the project took two hours to complete and required a few 1" x 10"'s and a sheet of ½" plywood for the front and back.

At thrift stores and the dime store in my neighborhood, I purchased marbles to fit into the small sockets Eric had made all around the butterfly opening. Before I installed the marbles with five-minute epoxy glue, I painted the whole cabinet, top and bottom.

For paint, I used some leftover interior latex house paint I had on hand, in yellow and blue. And I stamped meaningful words—"ideas," "dream," "create," and "believe"—to the doors and drawers. I finished by distressing or "aging" the paint by rubbing it with steel wool. I recommend a sealing topcoat of acrylic satin polyurethane. One to two coats will do.

butterflies are free

Kids who have grown up with support for their creativity are truly free to "become" whatever they can think up. Creative thinkers seem to always land on their feet, as well. If they can't find a job, they often make one. These self-starters and entrepreneurs believe they can help others, too, as they assume the roles of community activists and non-profit volunteers. Flying wherever their spirit leads them, the creatively empowered can travel the world on wings crafted in their childhood cocoons.

In a guided heart and hands project, I asked Margaret to think of what she is becoming in life and what she would like to unfold and develop within herself. She made a list. Then, we created a visual affirmation of those heart intentions: a painted and beaded butterfly pillow. As she applied the beads, I encouraged her to meditate on that which she intends to become: each bead put into place to symbolize her intentions to become more creative, courageous, and confident. In the back of her pillow, which was constructed by stepmom Laura, there is a pocket. Inside the pocket is an affirmation card that Margaret made listing her intentions. This all-in-one heart and hands project brings physical shape and substance to invisible thoughts, making the thoughts all the more real.

Andy and Laura, as usual, worked side-by-side with Margaret and me. Laura's skilled hands sewed ideas into place, while Andy helped with the upholstery and encouragement. Both stepmom and daughter teamed up to create some nifty projects of their own: a feathered mirror, jeweled pillows, painted windows, and an exotic canopy. Everyone collaborated together to fulfill Margaret's, and our own, butterfly dreams.

BUTTERFLY DREAMS: Over the year the author worked with Margaret and her parents, Margaret became more butterfly-like: self-reliant, confident, and freer to be herself.

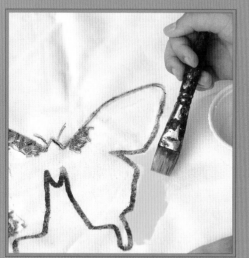

I AM BECOMING . . . BUTTERFLY PILLOW: Use the House of Belief pillow kit or draw your own butterfly outline. Sprinkle the beads on the glue-coated areas as you wish. (Do a sketch first to work out your ideas.) Allow drying time before moving the pillowcase. Make an intentions card and write—or have your child write what he/she dreams of becoming in life. Keep the intentions card in the pocket of your House of Belief pillow or slip it inside the zipper of your prefabricated pillow.

"i am becoming . . ." butterfly pillow

Who does your child want to become? What character traits will help your emerging butterfly to develop strong wings? Margaret declared that she is becoming more creative, confident and courageous. The *Butterfly Affirmation Pillow* will help your child to make these intentions visible so they are not forgotten.

HEART AND HANDS PROJECT

heart objective: Identify who you are becoming as you leave the cocoon of the past and unfold to your best self.

hands activity: Embellish the butterfly with beads and positive thoughts. As you decorate the butterfly, see it as yourself becoming all that you desire. Then take a step of acceptance. Fill out the affirmation card and write down your new positive intentions. Put it in the pocket for easy reference. Keep your pillow in view to uplift your mind and spirit. Expect to become all that you have stated.

steps to take: Detailed instructions under I am Becoming . . . Butterfly Pillow photos.

make an "in-memory" lamp

What is your child's core truth? What is the one powerful belief that he/she would like to keep in mind and in-memory? For our lamp, the one made by Margaret and me, the belief is one of resourcefulness. Its message is "What I need in life comes from my creative spirit—not my bank account." Our message is visually represented by the cast-off lamp and thrift store jewelry that adorns it. The lamp, like the proverbial light bulb going on, burns to remind us of the truth.

HEART AND HANDS PROJECT

heart objective: Create a statement of truth that you and your child would like to keep in memory.

hands activity: Adorn your lamp with whatever you can find. Or to make a jeweled lamp like ours, complete the following steps.

steps to take: Detailed instructions found under the Memory-In Lamp photos.

AN IN-MEMORY LAMP: After some fun afternoons spent cruising thrift stores, Margaret had plenty of jewelry to begin the decorating process. Using a low temperature hot glue gun, she secured her treasure in place.

CHAPTER 10

one sacred creativity

Many churches, mosques, and temples are cut from rare stone and layered in gold leaf. There are also inspiring stories told in stained glass and altars with objects for rituals and liturgies. Saints and other enlightened beings take form in statuary, in paintings, and in those colored windows. Music is an important part of the spiritual experience for many faiths. The faithful—those who commune together—congregate within the sanctuary, bound together by a common belief and the physical atmosphere of the shrine they have shared in creating.

In one small "temple" in the heart of the inner city, the congregants, though few, are mighty in their shared creativity and belief. Kiara Lewis, her mom, Gertie, and their friend Randee Werts have come together to create a sacred place that supports the 12-year-old's spiritual, mental, and emotional well-being. You won't find expensive materials, as Kiara and Gertie are Habitat for Humanity homeowners, but you will find that Kiara's sacred place is made of precious substances that exemplify her own creativity, belief, values, wishes, hopes, goals, and dreams for her life. She even created a shrine, in the form of a bulletin board, of her favorite recording artist Aaliyah, whose life and music reflected these same values.

NOTHING MORE SACRED: In Habitat homeowners Gertie and Kiara Lewis's home, they have learned the value of their creativity. "Nothing is more sacred than what comes from my heart and hands—and I am so happy my daughter has learned this early in life," says Gertie.

I first met Gertie and Kiara at a community workshop I was hosting for her Habitat for Humanity affiliate. Gertie was working on getting her "sweat equity" hours accomplished. Habitat homeowners buy their houses and offset their payments by spending as many as 500 hours working in their community and building their house or those of others. Gertie's story touched my heart. She had been homeless for a while. Since that time, she had been working hard to become a valued employee at a hospital and was now looking forward to owning her own home. She also had a hidden dream and passion: making and selling gift baskets. Through our work together, she has been able to make her "baskets of love," and her home even has a special closet area for her to pursue her small business.

Gertie describes what she learned at the House of Belief workshops:

I heard someone—Kelee—saying that I could make my dreams come true! That what was in my heart was real and important and that my hands could create it into reality. To know that my dream of a gift basket business could happen through my hands and creativity gave me so much hope. I want everyone to know about the Creator in them and to believe in their dreams. My Habitat house proves that miracles happen through creating and building with our hands.

Randee was also a participant in these workshops, a volunteer from the community who came to learn the House of Belief process so that she might teach and facilitate it to individuals and groups. I brought Randee and Gertie together for a belief partnership in which they would work to meaningfully decorate and improve each other's homes over a period of a year. The two women were a likely pairing. Both have hearts of gold and spirits of creativity to match.

A PERSONAL SHRINE: Kiara adds cut-out photos of the late singer Aaliyah to her shrine wall. Also included in her shrine are meaningful colors, symbols, and phrases.

precious materials

Randee started the process with Kiara where we started earlier, in Chapter Two, with Henry. Since limited financial resources were an important consideration in the Lewis home, as they are in most of our homes, an assessment of the true possessions and resources within the girl were vitally important. What were the riches stored in her heart, and how could these be used to create a place that was opulent with personal meaning?

Included in Kiara's wall collage are meaningful shadow boxes her friend Randee Werts helped her to create.

Here is what Randee found:

The design and decoration of Kiara's room has truly been a reflection of the changes she is experiencing as she moves from childhood to young womanhood—from Mickey Mouse to Aaliyah. Our beginning theme was around Mickey Mouse as a symbol of friendship, fun, humor, and openness. Then, almost overnight she transformed into a young woman and her role model became the pop singer Aaliyah.

Although, from our adult perspective, we may not always identify with our children's heroes and icons, we must learn to understand and respect them. The singer, Aaliyah—like The Beatles, The Supremes, The Clash, or any other teen idols were for us—has some very positive meanings for Kiara. Be sure and ask your own child what they find interesting about their pop icons, why they are inspiring, and what they represent to them, personally. Here is how Kiara describes Aaliyah:

She was so beautiful. Her life and songs are about love and being true to yourself. She was graceful and had a close relationship with her family. I want to be all of these things. I am so sad that she was killed in that plane crash, but it shows how a person lives on in their music.

Even through the tragedy of the singer's death, Kiara found inspiration. It seems this process of introspection and self-evaluation has empowered her to find the most positive lesson in any situation. To be conscious, and to put together the causes and outcomes of one's life choices, is essential in developing kids of strong character. To be able to think and identify what it is that one admires, and why, is fundamental in formulating a personal belief-system—a road map for your child to discover who they are and how they will successfully conduct their life. And this is the blueprint that serves in the building of a sanctuary within us.

my own "sacred shrine"

Randee introduced Kiara to one of her own favorite heart and hands projects: making a *Sacred Shrine*. When we think of such a thing, visions of an elaborate and expensive tribute sculpture or cabinet come to mind. In Randee's form of this, the precious materials come from within the creator of the shrine—their wishes, hopes, and dreams—not in the physical materials that make up the box.

Like most kids between 10 and 12 years old, Kiara is changing every day. Over the period of a year, she created two shrines with the help of her friend Randee. The first celebrated the friendly, kind character of Mickey Mouse.

belief partners

In the Lewis's neighborhood, the streets can be pretty mean. Every few blocks or so you can find firsthand examples of drug houses, robberies, and gang activity. But the Habitat homeowners are fighting to take their community back and make it safe and serene. Habitat sometimes builds houses in these war-torn areas because the building lots are either free or inexpensive. This is the benefit of having creative courage—you sometimes get things for free. This kind of courage empowers individuals to believe they can make a difference and that they possess the creativity to find a way to do so. For pre-teen girls, however, home must be a shield from the dangers that are all too close at hand, maybe even living on their block. Kiara shares her mother's point of view:

Momma doesn't even like for me to play outside. She is worried about what might happen. So, I stay in the house mostly. My room is really important because of this.

HEART AND HANDS PROJECT

heart objective: To create a focal point for you and/or your child's aspirations in life.

hands activity: Using a cigar box, shoebox, or even a bulletin board, create a representation of sacred wishes, hopes, goals, and dreams. Incorporate icons and role models. Also incorporate meaningful symbols, as well. For example, Kiara called upon the star symbol to represent the light shining from within herself and others.

ONE SACRED CREATIVITY

163

In helping Kiara construct a safe haven within her home, Gertie and Randee worked together for nearly a year. They committed to the project, and to each other, forming a belief partnership. Randee explains:

We shared time in one another's homes. Kiara learned to sew at my house and made most of the designs for the pillows for her bed. A major project at the Lewis home was preparing, priming, and painting the chest of drawers and bedside tables. We all learned some patience waiting for the enamel oil paint to dry. We were more than ready for the messy work to be done and everything to be beautiful. For me, it was a great creative experience to work with the pair, and to go through all of the ups and downs, together, kind of like a family.

This sacred circle of belief partners amplifies the old adage that "We are better together than we are apart." We all need support and encouragement, whether we are 9 or 49. By forming your own sacred circle of those people who believe in you and can work with you creatively, you will tap into the synergy of "true community." When we open our front doors to each other, we also open our hearts; and once inside, we find that we are pretty much the same. Within our homes and lives, we all want love, safety, purpose, family harmony, and friendships. Forming a sacred circle of belief promotes all of these individually and as a group. The House of Belief Studio is the center of my own sacred circle.

the house of belief studio

When I invite a child or an adult into my world of possibility—the House of Belief Studio—it starts a sequence of proactive steps in their lives. Simply by leaving the confines of their homes, and the limited thought patterns and experiences that can be embedded there, a porthole of new possibility is opened. A shift in consciousness occurs by entering a positive new space. Inside the studio, clients find heart and hand creativity, and a sacred circle of friendship.

PABLO'S IDEAL WORLD: To create a place where Pablo felt he truly belonged, he started by envisioning his ideal world. Here, he is a cartoonist—represented by his comic strip wallpaper. Also, "friends" are at the center of his life. He sleeps in a hammock, surrounded by the orange paint color he mixed himself. Below him is a trap door for easy escapes during his adventures in his handpainted gameboard floor mat.

When I first met Pablo Aguirre-Lagandré, he really needed a friend. The 11-year old had just moved to a new state and a new school. He was suffering as "the outsider" in his class. At times he didn't think he would make it through the initiation. This is what he told me:

They make fun of my name and that I am French. I really miss my old home and friends.
I feel like I don't belong here—or anywhere.

Pablo's mother Cecile and father Tedd were understandably concerned about him. The changes in his life were even taking a physical toll on him. Cecile described his school days:

Pablo gets sick a lot. He is so sensitive. The rejection is making him hurt inside and out. He
needs something that will help him adjust to the change, to give him back his confi-
dence and self-esteem.

I invited Pablo to come to the House of Belief studio. There, in a space all his own, he could create the changes he wanted in his world. Pablo first expressed his painful experiences, and then released them through healing heart and hands projects. By creating an "ideals" room, he was able to gain a whole new perspective about these life experiences.

a knight's quest

Like many boys his age, Pablo enjoys strategy games based on medieval stories. Arthurian legends, like the Grail quest, topped his list of interests. Here, we found a powerful modality for Pablo's healing. In discussing with Pablo the typical knight's quest, we noted that a man must face a lot of challenges. Often he finds himself in a foreign place surrounded by unfriendly hordes. The parallel wasn't lost on either of us and suddenly Pablo felt lionhearted. He too was on a quest to find his very own grail: the cup that legend says heals all who touch it.

In the analogy of Pablo's troubles and the knight's journey, we found a focal theme for his space. He would invent his own adventure game that would represent his quest and allow him to reconcile his painful experiences with meaningful outcomes. By elevating the trials of his life to the plot of a great story, he was able to see that challenges are a part of a knight's mission. Learning from life's twists and turns becomes the golden criteria for ultimately reaching a knight's destiny: the Holy Grail.

WINDOW ARMOR: Pablo and the author found what they needed for a resourceful window treatment at the local hardware store. A shade was made of reflective house insulation; and a rod to hang the vinyl shower curtains, fashioned from electrical conduit. Pablo wrapped the window trim in his favorite creative medium: duct tape.

the dark pit shortcut

Pablo decided to paint his game board on a floor cloth—a canvas mat. It would anchor and center his room. To illustrate the adventure, he painted a winding path with danger along the way: a giant vulture-like bird he calls the Demon Duck. Pablo explains:

In life everyone has a Demon Duck. It's a flaw that follows you around, your challenge to work through. Your Demon Duck will make you a stronger person in the end.

THE DARK PIT SHORTCUT: Pablo painted a floor mat as a game board for his own adventure game. The author, Pablo's brother, Yann, and his cousin Sam, visiting from Paris, helped him with his project.

Also, he painted a hazard, The Dark Pit Shortcut, which, I believe, is bravely self-referential. A real shortcut to healing. He said:

You see, I have connected the dark pit with a shortcut path directly to the finish or destination. Sometimes, you think you have fallen into a really bad place. But, later, you figure out it leads you to where you are supposed to be in life.

The young knight—and I am sure that with that last explanation, you will agree—just pulled the sword from the stone. A mythic sign that one is worthy to be part of the round table.

paint a "knight's quest" floor canvas

Pablo invites you and your child to join the round table by creating your own life quest adventure game. Start where we did: talk about life's challenges. Also, talk about the things that help you make it through hard times. Make a list. Create symbols for the challenges and the thoughts and experiences that give you courage and strength. Use these ideas and symbols on your game adventure and on game cards, too.

THE DARK PIT SHORTCUT: Pablo's self-made adventure game illustrates life's challenges and offers insights for surviving. His game cards attach positive affirmations to game symbols. For example: a flashlight represents his inner wisdom. A compass reminds him to remember his true north—who he really is, when he finds himself challenged.

HEART AND HANDS PROJECT

heart objective: To provide a mode of discussion, release, and learning for challenging and even painful experiences; and to find positive meaning in the adventure of life.

hands activity: On a primed canvas—heavy weight, start by drawing the pathway and symbols of your child's journey. Paint the images with acrylic paint. Finish with a clear coating of water-based acrylic. Also, on small canvas boards or even poster board cut to card-size, game cards featuring your child's hazard and power symbols. (See Pablo's game cards for ideas.)

TRAP DOOR ESCAPE: One of the features in Pablo's adventure game is a Trap Door Escape: a wooden box painted like a trap door. "You can store books in there—cause they help you escape," he says.

CONCLUSION

a storybook ending

As our real-life storybook nears its end, what comes to mind is one of the most enduring heroic legends of all time, The Knights of the Round Table. In calling together a *Kids' Sacred Circle,* we essentially form our own round table of those committed to heroic, belief-based creativity. Each of the kids in this book, and their families and friends committed to this heart and hands process, are part of our creative round table.

With his Arthurian wisdom, Pablo makes the perfect leader. His story provides us with the insight to view life's challenges as adventures—adventures best handled with creativity.

This is not your ordinary round table, however. There are your typical knights like Henry, who can defend a maiden's honor, and wizards like Alex, who can disarm a dark foe. But the table is also surrounded by other inspiring characters from our favorite stories, including: a magical school teacher; a frog-kissing princess; a velveteen baby; sisters from a Victorian novel; and a through-the-looking glass soul sister. What else would you expect from a *creative* round table, anyway?

Each of the knights on the following pages may express themselves differently, but be assured, they all go by the same creed. And their swords are colored pencils and paintbrushes. Each carries a paper shield—a personal Book of Belief. They live in fortified castles of their own making. When the evildoers come calling, our heroes have support systems and a positive strategy to keep them at bay. In fact, the bullies really have no chance at all—our knights having located the Holy Grail: *the belief and creativity that lives inside of each of them.*

A SAFE HAVEN: Kiara's room is her secure refuge from the dangers of the inner-city streets. Handmade pillows and recycled and thrift furniture, all made with limited financial resources, are symbols of her personal creative power in life. With the help of her mom and friend Randee, her Habitat house is now a home.

LION-HEARTED: In heroic fashion, Pablo, our roundtable leader, used duct tape to create his own suit of armor. More recently, Pablo has expanded his creative kingdom to include his interest in photography, cartooning, and music.

our kids' sacred circle

PROFILES

chapter one

Tommie Baughman, Jeanette Evans-Hamilton, and Ardis O. Petersen get in costume as a special agent, a bunny, and Ardis as the best character of all—herself. The trio created their own Kids' Sacred Circle, committing to use their creativity to make the world a better place for the kids in their city. Not Pictured: Kelly Edmister.

P
R
O
F
I
L
E
S

chapter two

Henry Burns and his mom, Stephanie, have recently sent their dogs Phoebe and Guinness to obedience school. It seems Phoebe is very creative and persistent in her efforts to escape their fence. Henry says, "When she jumps our fence she looks like a wonder dog being flown by her ears." And Henry himself is going to a neat new school, where the emphasis is on kindness, creativity, and leadership. Henry still continues to practice acts of kindness—often befriending kids with challenges.

Besides helping out Henry and the Berkovichs, Jackie Denning stays busy with many of her own art forms, including: painting, silkscreen, batik and textiles, and furniture making. "I really enjoy helping people to express something about their lives through the artwork I can do for them," she says. One of her favorite commissions is for pet portraits, because, like Henry and Stephanie, we all do love our pets.

chapter three

Jessica Collins loves attending St. Teresa's Academy. Her new self-esteem has helped her quickly develop a circle of friends. Still intent on becoming a marine biologist, she is studying hard toward that goal. She has added jewelry-making to her list of creative activities, making heart-felt "friendship" bracelets for the people she loves.

chapter four

Step-sisters Alexis and Anna are now fast friends. The two have learned to forgive, share—and even care about each other. From dance lessons to sports events, they enjoy spending time together. The two insist its time to simply call them "sisters."

chapter five

Beka and her dad, David Brown, are preparing to take on a new kind of creative project together, conveys her mom, Cherie. The "artwork" will be a vintage MGB sports car that will be Beka's to drive after the refurbishing. Beka has been doing all of the research on the parts needed. She says, "After creating my bedroom, I feel like I can do *anything*."

chapter six

Adopted baby Anna has now been with her family for two years, yet, it feels like they have been together forever. And she delights all who know her with her charm and wit. One day, when a fly came into her house and was pestering her, she shook her finger at it and exclaimed, *"Why don't you go home and find your mama?!"*

chapter seven

Our through-the-looking-glass soul sister Jasmine is writing almost everyday now. She has recently gone back to revise her story *The Life of Tina Francis June*, about a young girl who encounters racism and family hardship. She says, *"I don't always like what I write so sometimes I just throw it away."* My advice to her? Never throw your work away, just file it. Great-grandma Gloria agrees, *"Girl, you gotta respect your creative ideas."*

chapter eight

Alex is as ready for a sequel as his inspiration, Harry Potter. "Power-up—that's what I do when I need confidence," says Alex. Whether on the soccer field, basketball court, or in the classroom, Alex has become wizard-like. "My power comes from inside me and from the support of my family, especially my dad," he says. The foes are still out there, Harry would tell you that. But now, they haven't got a chance. Bullies *beware*.

chapter nine

No thrift store, no yard sale, no curbside pile of stuff is safe from the cocooning powers of Margaret and her family. Transforming lamps, chairs and sofas with the vision of decorative healers, the Rowzees use their creativity to turn cast-off caterpillars into butterflies. Margaret has taken the lesson to heart: "In life I can create what I need."

Margaret's mom, Susan, cultivated the creative potential in her daughter much like the flowers in her gardens. Flower blooms, like those in the paintings of Georgia O'Keefe, are an apt metaphor here. You see, O'Keefe's Ghost Ranch has been a family summer destination for years. At the ranch, families can choose from a variety of workshops guaranteed to nurture creativity and togetherness.

chapter ten

Kiara Lewis, Randee Werts, and Gertie Lewis glow with the radiant energy of shared creativity. "Working together over a year, we went through ups and downs kinda like a family," says Randee. Gertie adds, " There's a lot of love between us." Randee continues to share herself with those in need, participating in an art for Alzheimer's patients program. And Gertie's gift baskets bless all those they are bestowed upon.

photographer

"I have done a lot of good shooting in my checkered career," says our photographer Roy Inman—a "typically Roy" understatement by the man who snapped a famous photo of Abbey Hoffman, as well as others of JFK and Marilyn Monroe. Not to mention, great images and layouts for the **New York Times** and the **Wall Street Journal.** "But," he continues, "I have never done a project I believe in more than this one. When you give the creative power to kids and adults to transform their homes, they can transform their lives too."

mascot

Oliver Wendell, a bassett hound who claims the author as his human, has also become a teacher at the House of Belief Studio. He insists that he has the inside scoop on spiritual wisdom. Here are some of his teachings:

- **Be Affectionate**: Always run to the people you love;

- **Be Merciful**: Forgive people's mistakes in the time it takes to go outside and pooty. "Just, let it go," he says.

- **Be Joyful**: Play and cuddle more–watch TV less;

- **Be Goal-Oriented**: Chase the ball until you get it;

- **Be Grateful**: Never forget who rescued you from the pound.

form your own kids' sacred circle

Sewing Bees, quilting clubs, knitting groups, and craft guilds used to be an important part of village and town life, giving the participants a chance to bond through shared creativity. I invite you to form your own Kids' Sacred Circle: a group of kids or adults—or kids and adults together—that would like to share in the creative projects in this book, believing in and supporting one another. Your group could consist of friends and neighbors, or perhaps be part of a larger organization, such as a school class, club, or group; a faith-based organization like a church, temple, or synagogue; a nonprofit group like Habitat or other good cause; or a community-based group. Here is how to conduct your Kids' Sacred Circle:

- ✳ Find a designated meeting place or alternate houses. For example, "This week the circle is at my house and next week at yours." Or if you are using this idea in a school classroom, you have the benefit of a set location.

- ✳ Appoint a coordinator/leader(s). A partnership of two works well.

- ✳ Using the *Kids' Sacred Places* book or other House of Belief books, go chapter by chapter.

- ✳ Discuss the reading material and stories.

- ✳ Select heart and hands projects to do together or at home.

- ✳ Invite craftspeople and/or artists to demonstrate skills and techniques that relate to the heart and hands projects. Many of your circle members will have creative skills to share, as well.

- ✳ Be supportive, believing, and kind to one another.

- ✳ Limit your group size to 8 to 10 participants. If your class group is larger, divide it into two or three smaller groups of up to 10.

- ✳ Determine how materials will be paid for and who is responsible for the purchase of your materials.

✳ Be clear about your intentions: What are you all committing to do together? How many meetings will you have? How long will they be? What do you expect from them? How many times will you meet? I recommend an individual meeting length of two to three hours and that your group commit to three to four circle meetings together. If after the first set of meetings you would like to continue, then determine how many more you can commit to accomplishing.

✳ Register your Kids' Sacred Circle at our website www.houseofbelief.com. This will entitle your group to participate in national workshops and receive national workshop and conference discounts for tuition and other materials expenses.

With reminders of her wishes, hopes, and dreams close by, Kiara makes plans for a bright future.

RESOURCES

chapter one

ANY FABRIC & CREATIVITY STORE:
Walls, Furniture: acrylic paints, brushes
Bed Fringe
ANY PAINT STORE:
Acrylic wall paints
CREATIVE CONTRIBUTORS
ARDIS O. PETERSEN
Mural Artist/Drama Producer/Director
913.558.0197
TOMMIE BAUGHMAN
Faux Painting Artist
whatagr8morning@aol.com
JEANETTE EVANS-HAMILTON
President, European Faux Finishes LLC
816.616-3681

chapter two

ANY FABRIC & CREATIVITY STORE:

Curtain and bedspread 100% cotton sheeting

Headboard: foam core

Stencil: craft paper

Bed, curtains, and pillows: acrylic & fabric paints, brushes

Clock parts

Clock: canvas board

Book of Belief: paper, stamps, cord

ANY PAINT STORE:

Acrylic wall paints

CREATIVE CONTRIBUTORS

JIMMY SASSO

ARTtoGO.com

JACKIE DENNING

jackiedenningart.com

Artist: painting, printing, fabrics, furniture

727-443-7575

chapter three

ANY FABRIC & CREATIVITY STORE:

Mural: canvas, acrylic paint, markers

Chairs: canvas, stamps, markers, heat-transfer paper

Mosaics: Tumbled tile shards and stones

Walls: stamps

Book of Belief: Colored craft papers

RESOURCES

HOME AND OUTDOOR STORE (LIKE HOME DEPOT OR LOWE'S):
Mosaic table and pots: grout, tile, adhesive, sponge,
hammer, goggles,
Wall paint: acrylic

CREATIVE CONTRIBUTORS

JACKIE DENNING
jackiedenningart.com
Artist: painting, printing, fabrics, furniture
727-443-7575

chapter four

ANY FABRIC & CREATIVITY STORE:
Walls, pillows and lampshade: Silk daisies
Lampshade and swag kit
Fabrics: Dressing table skirt gingham and denim for screen and pillows
Bedspread tie-dye
Trimmings for screen and pillows
Fabric glue
Low temperature glue gun
Walls: acrylic paints

'70S LOVE CHAIR:
Retro Inferno Vintage and Modern Furniture (816.842. 4004)

chapter five

ANY FABRIC & CREATIVITY STORE:
Walls: assorted tissue paper
Headboard slipcover, bedding and pillows: satin, zebra, and metallic fabrics
Pillows: Poly-fil stuffing
Pillow stencils and acrylic paint and brushes
Window: spray adhesive for transparencies

CADILLAC PLASTICS (800.274.1000):

Window: colored Plexiglas chips

HOME AND OUTDOOR STORE (LIKE HOME DEPOT OR LOWE'S):

Walls: strippable pre-mixed wallpaper paste

Foam applicator chip brushes

Walls: acrylic paint

Window: key chain for colored squares

chapter six

ANY FABRIC & CREATIVITY STORE:

Duvet and pillows: cotton and chintz

Love Letter Blanket and pillows: Heat transfer paper for copier or scanner

Fabric paints

BELIEF WALL HANGING AND ANGEL MOBILE:

Peri Woltjer, Out Of My Mind Design

515-277-3002

periwoltjer@aol.com

chapter seven

ANY FABRIC & CREATIVITY STORE:

Mirror, paint

Chest: tissue paper, mirrors, adhesive, wood circles

Headboard and curtains: cotton fabrics

Lamp: Trimmings

Pillows: cotton muslin

Gift Boxes: cardboard boxes and paints, glitter, stamps, beads

Hero Pillows: Heat transfer paper for computer scanner

ANY PAINT STORE:

Acrylic Floor paint

STYROFOAM KIT BASE FOR HEADBOARD AND VALANCES:

CREATE IT DÉCOR

8102 E. Dale Lane

Scottsdale, AZ 85262

800.364.3088

createitdecor.com

HOME AND OUTDOOR STORE (LIKE HOME DEPOT OR LOWE'S):

An Eiffel Tower Lamp

ANY FABRIC & CREATIVITY STORE:

Colored Pillows and Comforter

chapter eight

HOME AND OUTDOOR STORE (LIKE HOME DEPOT OR LOWE'S):

Soccer Goal headboard

Lamp base and shade

Rug: artificial turf or indoor/outdoor

Wall paint

ANY FABRIC & CREATIVITY STORE:

Window: Vinyl Roller shade

Pillows: Acrylic Paints and stamps

chapter nine

ANY FABRIC & CREATIVITY STORE:

Curtains, bedding fabrics, pillow fabrics

Window Shade and Pillows: trimmings and beads

Window: Stained Glass paint

Pillows: Heat transfer paper for home scanner or copy machine

Window: paper for shade

Pillows and tassels: ribbons

ANY PAINT STORE:

Wall paint

chapter ten

house of belief studio

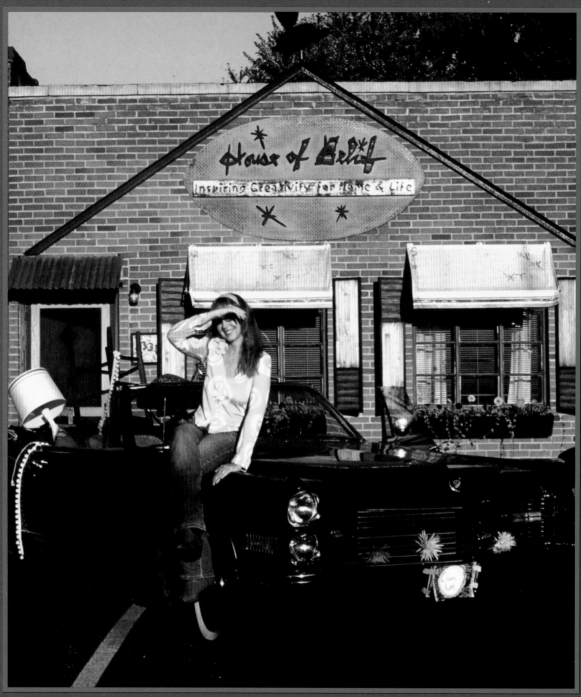

THE HOUSE OF BELIEF STUDIO: It is impossible to separate the meaning of the House of Belief™ brand from the story of the company's founder, Kelee Katillac.

About Kelee Katillac and House of Belief

While living in a rural Kansas trailer home 18 years ago, Katillac discovered that creating is believing. In the midst of a severe depression compounded by low income, low self-esteem, and disbelief in her own potential, Katillac somehow found the strength to begin expressing her creativity. The trailer house became symbolic of the process that would eventually heal her.

"One day I found a discarded chair on the sidewalk and it looked like I felt. The fabric was dirty and torn, the legs were loose. I began to restore it with whatever I could find. With every action of creativity I felt better and I began to believe more in my potential. Then, I made curtains for the trailer and painted the cabinets. I used fabric everywhere–all with very little money. I even made picture frames from the branches I found outside," says Katillac. " My heart used my hands to heal me. I eventually made my way into the world of interior design–but I knew I needed to share the lessons of my House of Belief."

The miraculous journey from a trailer house beginning to becoming an internationally-celebrated interior designer is introduced in the acclaimed book *House of Belief: Creating your Personal Style*. With no formal art or design training, her work is published in dozens of national magazines in which she illustrates that anyone can become creative through her belief-based design philosophy. She is also a frequent talk show guest demonstrating her heart & hands process to a national audience.

"Creative expression in our homes can give us a foundation of spiritual well being. The visual affirmation of a handmade home convinces us that what we can do for a chair, we can do for our whole lives. We begin to believe that, 'Yes, I can creatively heal a relationship; or creatively pursue a career goal; or creatively empower my children.'"

Katillac works with people from all walks of life. The company, **House of Belief™**, also partners with community volunteers to help limited-income homeowners and other at-risk groups to make their houses into homes. The therapeutic aspects of Katillac's heart & hand process creatively empowers participants to self-reliance and personal belief. At the House of Belief Studio, Katillac offers heart & hand therapy for those in transition. A portion of all House of Belief revenues benefit these charitable partnerships.

To find out more about Kelee Katillac workshops and seminars, and/or purchase books or products on-line:

www.housofbelief.com
House of Belief, P.O. Box 22716
Kansas City, Missouri 64113 Phone 816-756-1969
To contact Kelee Katillac: **kelee@houseofbelief.com**

ICEPRESS™ is the publishing division of The Institute for Creativity Empowerment

We at **The Institute for Creativity Empowerment** are honored to publish the book *Kids' Sacred Places: Rooms for Believing and Belonging* by Kelee Katillac. We feel it reflects our mission of empowering personal, family, community, corporate and global creativity. We hope this ICEPRESS book has benefited you in your quest for personal growth.

To order this or any of our other publications or to contact us:

www.ice-press.com
ICEPRESS P.O. Box 7128, Kansas City, Missouri 64113
Phone: 816-256-7012

more acclaim for kelee katillac and house of belief:

"...House of Belief offers inspiration for creating a beautiful and sacred space within the home."
– beliefnet.com

"Kelee encourages all of us to rekindle the creative spirit we were born with and make for ourselves a home that is not only a reflection of our beliefs ... but a haven in which to reaffirm what we value most."
– Lori L. Wilkinson, *Adventures Magazine*

"A book replete with ideas, photos, and exercises to help you unleash your creativity and make your living space an intimate part of who you are, a place to nurture your soul."
– Julia McBee, *The Atlanta Journal-Constitution*

"Interior decorating: more than just filling a room with stuff. It is bringing into form that which you see, feel, hear, experience and believe to be good and beautiful. There is no better guide for this journey than Kelee Katillac."
– Kingsley Hammet, DESIGNER/builder, *A Journal of the Human Environment*